Winter Gatherings

Winter Gatherings

Casual Food to Enjoy with Family and Friends

Rick Rodgers

Photographs by Ben Fink

WILLIAM MORROW

An Imprint of HarperCollins*Publishers*

HarperCollins books may be purchased for educational, business, or sales promotional use. For information please write: Special Markets Department, HarperCollins Publishers, 10 East 53rd Street, New York, NY 10022.

FIRST EDITION

Designed by Lorie Pagnozzi and Ashley Halsey

Library of Congress Cataloging-in-Publication Data
Rodgers, Rick, 1953–
    Winter gatherings : casual food to enjoy with family and friends / Rick Rodgers;
photographs by Ben Fink. — 1st ed.
        p.   cm.
    ISBN 978-0-06-167250-7
    1. Cookery, American. 2. Menus. 3. Title.
TX715.R7265   2009
641.5973—dc22

2008054282

09 10 11 12 13   OV/RRD   10 9 8 7 6 5 4 3 2 1

Acknowledgments

The acknowledgments in my books have a fairly constant cast of characters. We're a tightly knit group, and we easily manage to have a good amount of fun intermingled with the hard work it takes to get a cookbook between its covers.

This book marks the twentieth anniversary of my professional relationship with my literary agent, Susan Ginsburg. Coincidentally, we were friends for years before fate decreed that we work together. I wouldn't change one second of those years. Bethany Strout is Susan's wonderful assistant, and a constant help to both Susan and me.

At HarperCollins, thanks and thanks again to David Sweeney for developing the idea for a series of books on seasonal gatherings. It is an unique pleasure to work again with this book's editor, Stephanie Fraser. The production team at HarperCollins, from book designers Lorie Pagnozzi and Ashley Halsey to copy editor Sonia Greenbaum, is top-notch.

Once again, Diane Kniss cooked by my side, and made writing the book much more enjoyable than it had any right to be. And Patrick Fisher, my life partner, was there to taste, suggest, and wash dishes. (Between the two of them, Diane and Patrick must have washed enough of my dishes to sink a ship.) Ben Fink was responsible for the amazingly appetizing photography. He makes it look easy, but it takes an artist to continuously find new ways to bring food to life on paper. Thanks to Ben's partner, Joe Tully, for allowing a photo shoot at their home during the hectic holiday season. Arlene Ward and Josine Spina of Adventures in Cooking in Wayne, New Jersey, were generous in lending tableware for the photography. And finally, I lift a glass to my colleagues at *Bon Appétit* magazine, especially Barbara Fairchild and Kristine Kidd, who give me such a marvelous venue for trying out new recipes.

Contents

Introduction

When the weather turns cold, cooking becomes more of a challenge. Summer's juicy, sun-kissed bounty is long gone, and the remnants of the fall harvest have also dwindled. But that's fine by me. My mind turns to thoughts of woodsy mushrooms, earthy root vegetables and winter squashes with their inherent sweetness, bitter greens that can be tamed by long cooking, and the huge array of brightly colored citrus to be found at the market.

It's no secret that American cooks can get just about whatever produce they want out of its natural season—seasonability doesn't equate to availability anymore. And availability doesn't equate to quality, either. As you have surely found in your own experience, the more distant the source of your food, the less flavor it has. Do the math on the impact of long-traveled food on our environment and you are likely to lose your appetite. This isn't a book about only cooking with locally produced ingredients, although it has become a no-brainer that supporting your local agriculture is good for your community. But *Winter Gatherings*, like its companion volumes in this seasonal gatherings book series, does hope to inspire you to cook with traditional seasonal fare, and to show that your cooking will be the better for it.

"Traditional" is key here. When our country was agrarian-based, for the majority of cooks it was not just a struggle to get interesting fare on the table during the winter, but any food at all.

Fresh vegetables were pretty much restricted to root vegetables stored in the cellar. Canned, pickled, salted, and otherwise preserved produce and meats were eked out to create meals. Nowadays, we cook with turnips in January not because we don't have a choice, but because our palates crave the variety that cooking with the seasons brings.

Even though I don't have pantry shelves lined with rows of home-canned goods, I turn to plenty of preserved foods during the winter. Olives, anchovies, sauerkraut, canned and sun-dried tomatoes, chocolate, canned or dried beans, grains, cheese, maple syrup, and other foods that aren't "fresh," but certainly are tasty, are pulled into action.

As for fresh produce, the choices are more plentiful than might be expected. There are at least three growing regions (Southern California, the Southwest and Texas, and Florida) for winter citrus, so our fruit baskets can be loaded with oranges, lemons, and grapefruit, even when it's nippy outside. In winter, think of the vegetables that at one time would have been harvested late in the fall and stored in the root cellar for cooking—cabbage, leeks, onions, potatoes, turnips, rutabagas, sunchokes, apples, pears, carrots, parsnips, and more. In the summer, I savor every sip of gazpacho, but I don't enjoy my rutabaga and pear soup any less because the latter is made with more humble ingredients.

Chilly weather not only changes the ingredients we cook with, but how we cook them. Instead of quick meals cooked in a flash on the backyard grill, we cook hearty fare like stews and ragouts to warm the insides. I couldn't imagine serving sauerbraten with red cabbage and spaetzle any other time than December, January, or February, and it would be pretty silly to put braised lamb shanks with olives and feta on the menu in August. You may find yourself inside more during the winter, so dishes that require an occasional stir as they quietly simmer on the stove may be easier to attend to. Or it could be more primal, with our minds craving extra fat and carbohydrates to protect our bodies from the cold.

Winter is also the time for parties. Ancient cultures knew that the winter solstice signaled the beginning of the depletion of the food supply, so feasts were in order. The sumptuous bashes we throw for Christmas, Hanukkah, Kwanzaa, and New Year's have their roots in this millennium-old tradition. *Winter Gatherings* shares recipes for all kinds of meals, from modest weeknight suppers to holiday spreads. Food for other special occasions, from Super Bowl Sunday to Saint Valentine's Day to Mardi Gras, is included, too. I've included a few menus for some of the big events of the season, such as a Christmas Day dinner.

So, winter cooking does not have to mean an endless parade of potatoes. Let's lift our steaming mugs of hot chocolate and make a toast to the variety of foods that this austere, but ultimately flavorful, season has to offer.

Winter Gatherings

APPETIZERS AND BEVERAGES

Gruyère and Rosemary Gougères

Sweet and Spicy Chicken Wings

Dill–Whole Wheat Blini with American Caviar

Pizza with Fontina, Potatoes, and Tapenade

Baked Brie with Wild Mushrooms and Thyme

Gruyère and Cider Fondue

Chai Eggnog

Orange-Spice Hot Chocolate with Homemade Marshmallows

Gruyère and Rosemary Gougères

Makes about 2 dozen

These little savory cream puffs, perfect for snacking along with a glass of red wine, are great to have in your repertoire. Not only are they tasty, they can be made with ingredients you probably have on hand (yes, you can substitute another semifirm cheese, such as Cheddar or Fontina, for the Gruyère, and your favorite herb for the rosemary, as well) to whip up a quick fresh-from-the-oven appetizer for unexpected guests. There are a few little tricks to making gougères, which I've incorporated into the recipe. The French call this pastry *pâte à choux* (literally "cabbage pastry"), not just because the round puffs look like cabbages, but because this is the only pastry that is hot. That would make it *pâte à chaud* or "hot pastry," and *chaud* became corrupted into *choux* over the years.

¾ cup whole milk

6 tablespoons (¾ stick) unsalted butter, cut up

1 cup all-purpose flour

5 large eggs, divided

½ cup (2 ounces) shredded Gruyère cheese

2 teaspoons finely chopped fresh rosemary or 1 teaspoon crumbled dried rosemary

2 teaspoons Dijon mustard

½ teaspoon salt, plus more for the egg glaze

¼ teaspoon freshly ground black pepper

1. Position a rack in the center of the oven. Line a large baking sheet with parchment paper or a silicone baking mat.

2. Bring the milk and butter to a simmer in a heavy-bottomed medium saucepan over medium heat, stirring occasionally to be sure that the butter is completely melted by the time the milk simmers. Add the flour, all at once, and stir with a wooden spoon to make a thick paste. Reduce the heat to low. Stir constantly until the paste comes together into a ball and films the bottom of the saucepan, about 1 minute. Adjust the heat as necessary so the paste cooks without burning. The idea here is to force off excess moisture, in the form of steam, from the paste in order to make a crisper pastry. Remove the saucepan from the heat.

3. Whisk 4 of the eggs in a bowl to combine them. One-fourth at a time, stir the beaten eggs into the hot dough in the saucepan, and stir well until the dough comes together into a glossy mass. Stir in the Gruyère, rosemary, mustard, salt, and pepper.

4. Transfer the warm dough to a pastry bag fitted with a ½-inch plain tip. Pipe 24 walnut-sized balls of dough, about 1 inch apart, onto the baking sheet. Or drop the dough from a teaspoon onto the sheet. Beat the remaining egg well with a pinch of salt. Lightly brush some of the egg glaze on the mounds of dough, being sure that the egg does not drip down onto the sheet.

5. Bake until the balls are puffed and golden brown, 20 to 25 minutes. If the gougères have not baked long enough, they will deflate when taken from the oven, so bake for at least 20 minutes before checking them. Remove the sheet from the oven. Pierce each gougère with the tip of a small sharp knife. (This releases the steam from the interiors of the puffs and helps crisp them.) Return to the oven and continue baking until the gougères are crisp, 5 to 8 minutes. Let cool briefly on the baking sheet. (The gougères can be made up to 4 hours ahead. Reheat in a preheated 400°F oven until they are heated through, about 5 minutes.)

Sweet and Spicy Chicken Wings

Makes 6 to 8 servings

What's Super Bowl Sunday without a pile of jazzed-up chicken wings? These have become one of my favorite appetizers, as they couldn't be simpler to throw together, and they always disappear. I like the smoky high heat of the ground chipotle, but you could use milder, somewhat sweet ancho or hotter-than-hell habanero, if you prefer. Don't use the frozen "wingettes," however, because they give off too much liquid and don't crisp up nicely.

Vegetable oil for the baking sheet

4 pounds fresh (not thawed frozen) chicken "wingettes"

1½ teaspoons pure ground chipotle

1 teaspoon ground cumin

1 teaspoon kosher salt

3 tablespoons honey

1. Position a rack in the center of the oven and preheat to 425°F. Lightly oil a large rimmed baking sheet.

2. Put the chicken wings in a large bowl. Mix the chipotle, cumin, and salt together in a small bowl. Sprinkle over the wings, tossing well. Spread on the baking sheet.

3. Bake for 20 minutes. Turn the wings over and continue baking until golden brown and they show no sign of pink when pierced with the tip of a knife, about 25 minutes longer.

4. Transfer the wings to a large bowl. Pour off and discard the fat in the baking sheet. Drizzle the wings with the honey and toss. Spread again on the baking sheet and return to the oven. Bake until the wings are glazed with the honey, 5 to 10 minutes longer.

5. Transfer to a platter and serve hot, with a bowl for collecting the bones. (They're not very manly, but moist disposable towelettes of some kind would be welcome, too, as fingers will get sticky when eating these.)

Dill-Whole Wheat Blini with American Caviar

Makes 24 blini; 6 to 8 servings

Traditionally, imported caviar arrived in our country in November, but now, with the popularity and availability of American caviar, you don't have to wait for the cool weather to serve it. It remains one of the most elegant items to offer guests at New Year's. Some people wouldn't think of serving caviar without small buckwheat blini. Because buckwheat isn't the most common flour, I prefer to use whole wheat, which provides the whole grain flavor but will be used up much more quickly and not left to sit in the pantry.

BLINI

½ teaspoon dry active yeast

3 tablespoons warm (105° to 115°F) water

¾ cup whole milk

2 tablespoons unsalted butter, melted

2 tablespoons sour cream

1 large egg, separated

⅛ teaspoon sugar

⅛ teaspoon salt

½ cup all-purpose flour

½ cup whole wheat flour

2 teaspoons finely chopped fresh dill

Nonstick cooking spray for the skillet

2 ounces American caviar, such as black paddlefish

½ cup sour cream or crème fraîche

1. To make the blini, sprinkle the yeast over the warm water in a small bowl. Let stand until the mixture looks creamy, about 5 minutes. Stir to dissolve the yeast.

2. Whisk the milk, dissolved yeast, melted butter, sour cream, egg yolk, sugar, and salt together in a medium bowl until combined. Add the flour and whole wheat flour, and whisk until smooth. Cover with plastic wrap and let stand at room temperature until bubbly (it will not double in volume), about 2 hours.

3. Whisk the egg white in a greaseproof small bowl until soft peaks form. Add to the batter, along with the dill, and fold together.

4. When ready to serve, heat a griddle or large skillet over medium-high heat until a sprinkle of water splashed on the surface forms skittering beads. Reduce the heat to medium-low. Using a heaping tablespoon for each blini, spoon the batter onto the griddle. Cook until holes appear in the tops of the blini, about 1 minute. Turn and cook until the other sides are golden brown, about 30 seconds. Transfer to a platter lined with a clean, fragrance-free napkin or kitchen towel, and wrap the blini in the towel to keep warm while making the remaining blini. (The blini are best freshly made. They can be made up to 2 hours ahead and stored at room temperature. To reheat, overlap blini on a large baking sheet and bake in a preheated 350°F oven, uncovered, until hot, about 5 minutes.)

5. Serve the blini, accompanied by bowls of caviar and sour cream. Allow guests to top each blini with the caviar and sour cream.

Pizza with Fontina, Potatoes, and Tapenade

Makes 4 servings

Knowing how to make homemade pizza is a great skill to have because you are in charge of the toppings and their quality. While I have friends who are capable of churning out pizza after pizza for a crowd, I prefer to serve a single pizza as an appetizer. This vegetable pizza combines the mellow flavors of Fontina cheese and potatoes with bold accents of olive tapenade—much different than a summery tomato-and-basil pizza, but just as good in its own way. To give the pizza its crisp golden brown crust, use a pizza stone and paddle.

PIZZA DOUGH
1 (¼-ounce) package active dry yeast (2¼ teaspoons)

¼ cup warm (105° to 115°F) water

3 tablespoons extra-virgin olive oil, divided

2 cups bread flour

1 teaspoon salt

½ cup cold water, as needed

GARLIC OIL
3 tablespoons extra-virgin olive oil

2 garlic cloves, finely chopped

3 small Yukon gold potatoes (8 ounces total), scrubbed but unpeeled

Cornmeal for the pizza paddle

⅓ cup freshly grated Parmesan

1½ cups (6 ounces) shredded Italian Fontina d'Aosta

1 bottled roasted red bell pepper, drained, seeded, and coarsely chopped

3 tablespoons tapenade (see Note)

2 teaspoons finely chopped fresh rosemary

Crushed hot red pepper flakes

1. To make the pizza dough, sprinkle the yeast over the warm water in a small bowl. Let stand 5 minutes; stir until dissolved. Add 2 tablespoons of the olive oil.

2. Place the flour and salt in a food processor fitted with the metal chopping blade and pulse briefly to combine. Add the yeast mixture. With the machine running, gradually add enough cold water through the feed tube until the mixture comes together in a ball on top of the blade. Process to knead for 45 seconds. Gather up the dough and briefly knead by hand on a lightly floured work surface.

3. Pour the remaining 1 tablespoon oil into a medium bowl. Add the dough and turn to coat liberally with oil. Cover with plastic wrap and let stand at room temperature until doubled in volume, about 1¼ hours.

4. To make the garlic oil, heat the oil and garlic in a small saucepan over low heat until the oil bubbles around the garlic, about 3 minutes. Remove from the heat and let cool.

5. Place the potatoes in a medium saucepan and add enough salted water to cover. Cover with a lid and bring to a boil over high heat. Reduce the heat to medium and cook with the lid ajar until the potatoes are almost tender when pierced with a small

knife, 12 to 15 minutes. Drain and let cool until easy to handle. Using a thin knife, slice the potatoes into ⅛-inch-thick rounds. Spread the potato rounds on a plate and lightly brush the tops with the garlic oil. Reserve the remaining garlic oil.

6. Position a rack in the lower third of the oven. Place a pizza stone on the rack and preheat the oven to 450°F.

7. Punch the dough down and transfer to a floured work surface. Roll, pat, and stretch the dough into a 12- to 14-inch round. Sprinkle a pizza paddle liberally with cornmeal. Transfer the dough round to the paddle and reshape as needed. Cover loosely with plastic wrap and let stand for 10 minutes.

8. Sprinkle the dough with the Parmesan and ½ cup of the Fontina. Arrange the potato slices, oiled side up, on the dough, leaving a 1-inch border around the edge. Sprinkle with the roasted red pepper. Drop heaping ¼ teaspoons of tapenade over the pizza. Sprinkle with the remaining 1 cup Fontina. Lightly brush the exposed dough border with garlic oil.

9. Slide the pizza off the paddle onto the hot pizza stone. Bake until the underside is deep golden brown (using the paddle to lift the pizza and check), 15 to 20 minutes. Slip the paddle under the pizza and transfer to a cutting board. Spoon the remaining chopped garlic and its oil over the pizza to taste. Sprinkle with salt, rosemary, and red pepper flakes to taste. Cut into wedges and serve hot.

Note

Tapenade, a savory spread made from olives, anchovies, garlic, and herbs, is available at specialty grocers and many supermarkets. Olivada, an olive spread that does not usually include anchovies, is a good substitute. Or simply scatter ½ cup pitted and coarsely chopped black Mediterranean olives over the pizza.

Baked Brie with Wild Mushrooms and Thyme

Here is a nigh-perfect appetizer to serve with red wine on a cool evening—earthy mushrooms served over melting Brie to spread on crusty bread. You'll need a medium-size edible-rind cheese, such as Brie de Colummiers or imported or domestic Camembert, that is sold in a wooden box, as the box will contain the cheese while it heats in the oven. For a large crowd, use a large wheel of cheese and triple the topping.

Mushroom Topping

½ ounce dried porcini mushrooms

⅔ cup hearty red wine, such as a Cabernet/Shiraz blend

2 tablespoons unsalted butter

6 ounces cremini mushrooms, halved or quartered

6 ounces shiitake mushrooms, stemmed, caps sliced

2 tablespoons minced shallots

2 teaspoons chopped fresh thyme

Salt and freshly ground black pepper

One (14-ounce) ripe Brie in a wooden box, such as Brie de Colummiers
    (about 5 inches in diameter)

1 baguette, cut into ¼-inch-thick slices

1. For the mushrooms, rinse the porcini in a wire sieve under cold water to remove any dirt. Bring the wine to a simmer in a small saucepan over low heat. Remove from the heat, add the porcini, and let stand until the mushrooms soften, about 20 minutes. Lift the mushrooms from the wine and coarsely chop them. Strain the wine through a wire sieve lined with moistened paper towels into a small bowl. Reserve the wine.

2. Melt the butter in a large skillet over medium-high heat. Add the cremini and shiitake mushrooms and cook, stirring occasionally, until they begin to brown, about 8 minutes. Add the shallots and stir until softened, about 1 minute. Stir in the soaked porcini and the strained wine. Bring to a boil and cook until the wine is almost completely evaporated, about 5 minutes. Stir in the thyme. Season with salt and pepper. Remove from the heat and let cool. (The mushrooms can be made up to 1 day ahead, cooled, covered, and refrigerated. Bring to room temperature before proceeding.)

3. Remove the Brie from the box, reserving the bottom half of the box. Using a sharp knife, cut off and discard the top rind from the cheese. Return the cheese to the bottom half of the box, cut side up. Mound the mushrooms on top of the cheese. Place the box with the cheese and mushrooms on a baking sheet. (The cheese can be prepared and refrigerated up to 8 hours before baking.)

4. Position a rack in the center of the oven and preheat to 350°F. Bake until the cheese begins to melt, about 15 minutes. Transfer the cheese in its box to a serving platter. Serve hot, with baguette slices, allowing guests to scoop and spread the cheese and mushrooms onto the bread.

Gruyère and Cider Fondue

Many people serve fondue as a meal, but it is also a lovely appetizer to serve with a light-bodied red wine. Just the sight of a fondue pot over a low flame is bound to warm the insides even before a single bread cube is speared. One thing to remember: a fondue pot is meant to serve, but not actually cook, the fondue, which is best made on the stove.

1 cup hard apple or pear cider

1 tablespoon cider vinegar

4 cups (1 pound) shredded Gruyère

1 tablespoon plus 2 teaspoons cornstarch

1 tablespoon Calvados, applejack, or Poire William

Freshly ground black pepper

Cubes of crusty bread, cored and sliced Granny Smith apples or Bosc pears, and sliced grilled kielbasa, for serving

1. Combine the cider and vinegar in a nonreactive medium saucepan. Stirring to dissipate the bubbles, bring to a simmer over medium heat. Reduce the heat to medium-low; the liquid should barely simmer.

2. Toss the Gruyère with the cornstarch in a large bowl to coat the cheese. A handful at a time, whisk the cheese into the simmering cider mixture, whisking until the first

batch is melted before adding more. When all the cheese has been added, return the heat to medium and heat just until the fondue bubbles a few times; do not overcook. Remove from the heat and stir in the Calvados. Season with pepper.

3. Transfer to a fondue pot set on its trivet over the flame. Arrange the bread, apples, and sausage for dipping on a platter. Serve the fondue hot with fondue forks and the platter of dipping ingredients.

Chai Eggnog

I consider it a crime to go through December without at least one glass of eggnog. As it is a staple of the holiday party menu, most recipes are for a crowd, but this makes just enough for a few friends—you can always multiply the ingredients for a larger batch. This recipe came to me when I was sipping a hot glass of aromatic chai, and noted that the combination of spices reminded me of gingerbread, so they would translate beautifully into that winter specialty, eggnog. It doesn't have any liquor in it, but some dark rum wouldn't be amiss.

2 cups heavy cream

Three 3-inch cinnamon sticks

1 teaspoon black peppercorns

9 green cardamom pods, crushed

9 quarter-sized slices fresh ginger

1 teaspoon whole cloves

4 orange pekoe or Darjeeling tea bags

3 large eggs, separated

⅔ cup sugar

1. Combine the cream, cinnamon, peppercorns, cardamom, ginger, and cloves in a small saucepan over medium heat. Remove from the heat and add the tea bags. Let stand for 5 minutes. Strain through a wire sieve into a heatproof bowl, pressing hard on the tea bags. Let cool completely.

2. Beat the egg yolks and sugar in a medium bowl with an electric mixer on high speed until the mixture is thickened and pale yellow. On low speed, beat in the cream mixture.

3. Using clean beaters, beat the egg whites in a greaseproof medium bowl with the mixer on high speed until soft peaks form. Fold the whites into the yolk mixture. Cover and refrigerate until chilled, at least 2 and up to 12 hours. Serve chilled.

A Festive Christmas Dinner

Gruyère and Rosemary Gougères (page 2)

Chai Eggnog (opposite)

Mussel and Fennel Bisque (page 41)

Rib Roast with Blue Cheese Crust (page 68)

Potato and Garlic Gratin (page 126)

Fresh green beans sautéed

with shallots

Pear Soufflés "Hélène" (page 155)

Orange-Spice Hot Chocolate with Homemade Marshmallows

Makes 4 servings

This is a very grown-up version of that childhood favorite, hot chocolate topped with marshmallows. Most hot chocolate drinks are actually made with cocoa. I prefer this method, which allows me to enjoy the flavor of my favorite eating chocolate. For my taste, I like a semisweet chocolate with about 55% cacao solids (you'll find this listed on the label of the best brands), but you may vote for a more bitter variety. And if you are a purist, leave out the orange zest and cinnamon, but I think that they add an irresistible wintry aroma and flavor. And, of course, the Homemade Marshmallows make it very special indeed.

8 ounces high-quality bittersweet chocolate, coarsely chopped

3 cups milk

Zest of 1 orange, removed in strips with a vegetable peeler

Two 3-inch cinnamon sticks

8 to 12 Homemade Marshmallows (page 142)

1. Bring 1 cup of water to a boil in a small saucepan. Remove from the heat, add the chocolate, and let stand for 3 minutes. Whisk until smooth.

2. Bring the milk, orange zest, and cinnamon to a simmer in a medium saucepan over medium-low heat. Remove from the heat and let stand for 5 minutes. Using a slotted spoon, remove and discard the orange zest and cinnamon. Add the melted chocolate and whisk well. Reheat, whisking constantly, until piping hot.

3. Ladle into 4 large mugs and top each with 2 or 3 marshmallows. Serve immediately.

SOUPS AND SALADS

Rutabaga and Pear Soup

Escarole and Farro Soup

Jerusalem Artichoke and Mushroom Soup

Chicken, Potato, and Leek Soup

"Stuffed Cabbage" Soup

Moroccan Lamb and Garbanzo Bean Soup

Mussel and Fennel Bisque

Lime and Cilantro Slaw

Roasted Beet and Orange Salad

Poached Leeks with Creamy Vinaigrette

Rutabaga and Pear Soup

This may sound like an odd combination, but it has become one of my favorite soups for entertaining. Expect a wonderful blend of earthy, sweet flavors from the interplay of rutabaga and pears. And with its deep golden color, this soup visually brightens up a cold winter night.

3 tablespoons unsalted butter, divided

⅔ cup chopped shallots

2½ pounds rutabaga (otherwise known as waxed yellow turnip),
   peeled and cut into 1-inch cubes

6 cups chicken stock, preferably homemade, or use canned low-sodium broth

3 ripe Comice pears, peeled, cored, and cut into ½-inch dice

1½ teaspoons chopped fresh thyme

Salt and freshly ground black pepper

1. Melt 2 tablespoons of the butter in a large saucepan over medium heat. Add the shallots and cook, stirring often, until tender, about 3 minutes. Add the rutabaga and stir well. Add the stock and bring to a boil over high heat. Reduce the heat to medium-low and cover. Simmer until the rutabaga is tender, about 45 minutes.

2. Meanwhile, melt the remaining 1 tablespoon butter in a large nonstick skillet over medium-high heat until the foam subsides. Add the pears and cook, stirring occasionally, until lightly browned, about 5 minutes. Transfer about one-third of the pears to a bowl to use as garnish.

3. Add the thyme and the remaining pears to the soup, and simmer for 5 minutes. In batches, puree the soup in a blender. Return to the pot and season with salt and pepper to taste. Serve hot, in individual bowls, each garnished with a spoonful of the reserved pears.

Turnips and Rutabagas

Most cooks consider root vegetables to be humble ingredients, and turnips and rutabagas have been relegated to the lowest rung. Unimpressive in appearance, their pungent flavor more than makes up for their bland looks. The cabbagelike aroma is a defense mechanism in the plants, but it doesn't discourage intrepid cooks.

I look forward to using these two vegetables to add spark to my winter cooking. They are most popular when combined with other ingredients to balance their more sulfurous aromas. I often cook them with apples and pears to bring a touch of sweetness, or with starchy potatoes to give them extra body.

Turnips aren't only appreciated for the bulbous roots, but also for their peppery green tops. The tops are usually trimmed and sold separately. New greens will continue to sprout from the turnips. Turnips with tiny sprouting greens will be older, and their sharpness will be well developed.

Also called Swedes or yellow or waxed turnips, rutabagas are actually a cross between regular turnips and a wild cabbage. They can grow to an admirable girth, and their skins are often shellacked with thick wax to give them a longer shelf life. Rutabagas are very popular in New England, and many a holiday meal isn't considered complete without mashed "turnips." However, when I have tried to make my favorite rutabaga dishes on the West Coast with small, unwaxed rutabagas, I have found them impossible to cook to tenderness, even after boiling for hours. This could be because rutabagas become pithy and hard when grown during warm weather. So hold out for "authentic" big old rutabagas grown in cold climes.

Escarole and Farro Soup

Makes 6 to 8 servings

This satisfying soup is similar to minestrone and other rustic Italian soups. Often I'll start the soup by sautéing a few ounces of chopped pancetta or prosciutto in the oil before adding the vegetables, but it really isn't necessary. Think ahead with the farro, which is similar to wheat berries, and soak it overnight before cooking to reduce the cooking time.

¾ cup farro (see Note)

2 tablespoons olive oil

1 medium yellow onion, chopped

2 medium carrots, chopped

2 celery ribs, chopped

2 garlic cloves, finely chopped

6 cups chicken stock, preferably homemade, or use low-sodium canned broth

One 14½-ounce can diced tomatoes, with juice

One 12-ounce head escarole, well rinsed, hard stems removed, and coarsely chopped

Salt and freshly ground black pepper

Chopped fresh parsley, for serving

Freshly grated Parmesan, for serving

---

1. The night before making the soup, put the farro in a bowl and add enough cold water to cover by 1 inch. Let stand in a cool place or refrigerate for at least 12 hours.

2. Drain the farro in a wire sieve. Bring a medium saucepan of lightly salted water to a boil over high heat. Add the farro and reduce the heat to medium-low. Simmer until the farro is tender, about 30 minutes. Drain the farro and set aside.

3. Meanwhile, heat the oil in a large pot over medium heat. Add the onion, carrots, and celery and cook, stirring occasionally, until softened, about 5 minutes. Stir in the garlic and cook until it gives off its fragrance, about 1 minute. Stir in the stock and the tomatoes with their juice. Bring to a boil over high heat. Reduce the heat to medium-low and simmer for 45 minutes.

4. Add the cooked farro and escarole. Cook, stirring occasionally, until the escarole is very tender, about 15 minutes. Season with salt and pepper to taste.

5. Serve hot, sprinkling each serving with parsley, and with the cheese on the side.

Note

Farro is a very old type of wheat that is still grown, as it has been for centuries, in Italy. It is very similar to wheat berries, which can be substituted.

Jerusalem Artichoke and Mushroom Soup

Makes 6 servings

Never underestimate the element of surprise in your menus—it is always interesting to expose your guests to new ingredients. Also known as sunchokes, Jerusalem artichokes are hardly new, but they aren't as popular as they could be, and most guests will be guessing at this soup's main ingredient. Their earthiness pairs nicely with mushrooms, and the soup is never better than when enjoyed with a glass of Pinot Noir.

4 tablespoons olive oil, divided

2 pounds Jerusalem artichokes, peeled and cut crosswise into ¼-inch-thick slices

1 large onion, chopped

2 garlic cloves, finely chopped

1 teaspoon finely chopped fresh rosemary, plus more for garnish,
    or ½ teaspoon crumbled dried rosemary

6 cups chicken stock, preferably homemade, or use canned low-sodium broth

10 ounces cremini mushrooms, sliced

Salt and freshly ground black pepper

1. Heat 2 tablespoons of the oil in a large pot over medium heat. Add the Jerusalem artichokes and cook, stirring occasionally, until golden brown, abut 10 minutes.

2. Add the onion and cook, stirring occasionally, until it softens, about 5 minutes. Stir in the garlic and rosemary, and cook until the garlic gives off its fragrance, about 1 minute. Stir in the stock and bring to a boil. Reduce the heat to medium-low. Simmer until the artichokes are barely tender, about 20 minutes.

3. Heat the remaining 2 tablespoons oil in a large skillet over medium-high heat. Add the mushrooms and cook, stirring occasionally, until they are lightly browned, about 6 minutes. Stir into the soup and cook until the artichokes are very tender, about 10 minutes more. Season with salt and pepper to taste.

4. Serve hot, topping each serving with a sprinkle of fresh rosemary.

Chicken, Potato, and Leek Soup

The trio of chicken, potatoes, and leeks has often been turned into soup, but most cooks go for a delicate version that is one step away from being vichyssoise. This one is much more robust and appropriate for a winter meal, almost like roast chicken in a bowl. The soup has plenty of flavor with water alone, but use chicken stock if you prefer it.

4 bacon slices, coarsely chopped

2 teaspoons vegetable oil

Two 12-ounce chicken breast halves with skin and bone

2 tablespoons unsalted butter

3 large leeks, white and pale green parts only, chopped (about 2 cups)

8 cups water (or substitute chicken stock if you prefer)

1 large baking potato, such as russet or Burbank, peeled and diced

1 teaspoon finely chopped fresh thyme or ¾ teaspoon dried thyme

½ cup heavy cream

Salt and freshly ground black pepper

1. Cook the bacon and oil together in a large saucepan over medium heat, stirring occasionally, until crisp and browned, about 8 minutes. Using a slotted spoon, transfer the bacon to paper towels to drain, leaving the fat in the saucepan.

2. Add the chicken to the fat, skin side down. Cook until the skin is deeply browned, about 4 minutes. Turn and cook the other side until lightly browned, about 2 minutes. Transfer to a plate.

3. Pour off any fat in the saucepan. Add the butter to the saucepan and return to medium heat. Add the leeks and cook, stirring occasionally, scraping up any browned bits in the bottom of the saucepan, until tender, about 8 minutes. Stir in the water with the potato and thyme. Return the chicken to the saucepan and bring to a boil. Reduce the heat to medium-low. Simmer until the chicken is cooked through and the potato is tender, about 25 minutes.

4. Transfer the chicken to a cutting board. Remove the skin and bones and coarsely chop the meat. Set aside.

5. Add the cream to the soup and heat until piping hot, but do not boil. Season with salt and pepper to taste. In batches, puree the soup in a blender and return to the saucepan.

6. Serve hot, topping each serving with some of the chicken and bacon.

"Stuffed Cabbage" Soup

When I first moved to New York, I lived in the East Village, which was dotted with Eastern European coffee shops. Each place featured stuffed cabbage as a cheap daily special, and I quickly learned to both love it and make my own. When I don't have the time for rolling and stuffing the cabbage, I make this soup that has all of the flavors, but is less labor-intensive.

Meatballs

1 large egg

3 tablespoons dried unflavored bread crumbs

1 teaspoon salt

½ teaspoon freshly ground black pepper

1 pound ground round beef

2 tablespoons vegetable oil

Soup

1 tablespoon vegetable oil

1 large onion, chopped

2 carrots, chopped

2 celery ribs, chopped

2 garlic cloves, finely chopped

4 cups packed coarsely chopped green cabbage (about 1 pound)

4 cups beef stock, preferably homemade, or use low-sodium canned broth

One 28-ounce can crushed tomatoes in puree

2 cups water

½ teaspoon dried thyme

2 tablespoons sugar

2 tablespoons cider vinegar

1 bay leaf

⅓ cup long-grain rice

Salt and freshly ground black pepper

Sour cream, for serving

1. To make the meatballs, beat the egg in a medium bowl. Add the bread crumbs, salt, and pepper and mix together. Add the beef and mix lightly but thoroughly with your hands. Roll into 16 meatballs.

2. Heat the oil in a large pot over medium-high heat. In batches, add the meatballs and cook, turning occasionally, until browned, about 5 minutes. Using a slotted spoon, transfer to a plate, leaving the fat in the pot.

3. To make the soup, add the oil to the fat in the pot. Add the onion, carrots, and celery and cook, stirring occasionally, until softened, about 5 minutes. Stir in the garlic and cook until it gives off its fragrance, about 1 minute. Add the cabbage and stir well. Add the stock, tomatoes and their puree, water, thyme, sugar, vinegar, and bay leaf, and bring to a boil. Reduce the heat to medium-low and simmer for 30 minutes. Add the meatballs and cook until they show no sign of pink when pierced in the center, about 15 minutes.

4. Meanwhile, bring a medium saucepan of salted water to a boil over high heat. Add the rice and reduce the heat to medium-low. Simmer until the rice is tender, about 20 minutes. Drain in a wire sieve and rinse under cold running water.

5. Stir the cooked rice into the soup. Season with salt and pepper to taste.

6. Serve hot, with a dollop of sour cream on each serving.

Variation

Meaty Beet Borscht: Add 3 medium beets, peeled and cut into ½-inch dice, to the soup with the stock. Simmer until the beets are tender, about 45 minutes, before adding the browned meatballs. If you wish, substitute 2 tablespoons chopped fresh dill for the dried thyme.

Moroccan Lamb and Garbanzo Bean Soup

Makes 6 to 8 servings

Moroccan cooks are masterful at blending spices, as this fragrant and deeply flavored soup attests. Originally this soup was made with chunks of boneless lamb shoulder roast, but unfortunately that cut is very hard to find at supermarkets. I now use lamb chops, and their bones also enrich the broth.

1 teaspoon coriander seeds

1 teaspoon cumin seeds

¼ teaspoon ground cinnamon

¼ teaspoon crushed hot red pepper flakes

Three 12-ounce lamb shoulder chops, cut about ¾ inch thick

Salt and freshly ground black pepper

3 tablespoons olive oil, divided

1 medium onion, chopped

2 garlic cloves, finely chopped

2 cups chicken stock, preferably homemade, or use canned low-sodium broth

One 28-ounce can plum tomatoes in juice, coarsely chopped, juice reserved

2 cups water

One 15- to 19-ounce can garbanzo beans (chickpeas), drained and rinsed

Chopped fresh cilantro, for garnish

1. Heat a small skillet over medium heat. Add the coriander and cumin seeds and cook, stirring occasionally, until the seeds are toasted and fragrant. Transfer to a plate and let cool. Transfer to an electric spice grinder or a mortar and grind into a coarse powder. Stir in the cinnamon and red pepper flakes. Set aside.

2. Cut the meat from the chops, trimming away excess fat, and cut the meat into bite-size pieces. Reserve the bones. Season the meat with salt and pepper.

3. Heat 1 tablespoon of the oil in a large pot over medium-high heat. Add the lamb and cook, stirring occasionally, until lightly browned, about 4 minutes. Using a slotted spoon, transfer the meat to a plate, leaving the fat in the pan.

4. Add the remaining 2 tablespoons oil to the pot and heat. Add the onion and reduce the heat to medium. Cook until softened, about 3 minutes. Stir in the garlic and cook until it gives off its fragrance, about 1 minute. Stir in the spice mixture and cook until it gives off its aroma, about 15 seconds. Pour in the stock and scrape up the browned bits in the pot with a wooden spatula. Return the meat and bones to the pot, along with the tomatoes and their juice and the water. Bring to a boil over high heat, skimming off any foam that rises to the surface. Reduce the heat to medium-low and simmer until the meat is tender, about 1 hour. Add the beans and cook until heated through, about 10 minutes. Season with salt and pepper to taste. Remove and discard the lamb bones.

5. Serve hot, sprinkling each serving with cilantro.

Mussel and Fennel Bisque

Makes 6 servings

Poor fennel—it just doesn't get its due from American cooks. Here, it lends its light anise flavor to a creamy bisque that is elegant enough to serve to company, yet comforting enough to serve for a supper or lunch.

2 pounds mussels

1 cup dry white wine

4 cups homemade fish stock or bottled clam juice, as needed

1 large head fennel (also known as anise), preferably with fronds

3 tablespoons unsalted butter

¼ cup chopped carrots

½ cup chopped shallots

¼ cup long-grain rice

1 teaspoon tomato paste

¼ teaspoon dried thyme

1 bay leaf

Salt and freshly ground black pepper

1 cup heavy cream

Chopped fresh parsley, for garnish (optional)

1. Scrub the mussels under cold running water, debearding them, if necessary. Put the mussels in a large bowl and add enough cold salted water to cover. Let stand for 1 to 2 hours. Drain and rinse the mussels.

2. Combine the mussels and wine in a large saucepan and cover. Bring to a boil over high heat. Cook, shaking the pan occasionally, until all of the mussels open, about 5 minutes. Using tongs, transfer the mussels to a bowl. Discard any unopened mussels.

3. Strain the cooking liquid through a wire sieve lined with moistened, wrung-out cheesecloth to remove any grit. Add enough fish stock or clam juice to the mussel liquid to make 5 cups. (If you run out of stock or clam juice, use water.) Remove the mussels from their shells and place the meat in a bowl, discarding the shells. Cover and refrigerate the shelled mussels.

4. If the fennel has its fronds attached, remove, finely chop, and reserve them for garnish. Cut the fennel bulb in half lengthwise and cut out and discard the hard triangular core. Cut the fennel into ½-inch dice; you should have about 2¼ cups fennel.

5. Heat 2 tablespoons of the butter in a large saucepan over medium heat. Add 1½ cups of the chopped fennel and the carrots. Cover and cook, stirring occasionally, until softened, about 10 minutes. Stir in the shallots and cook, uncovered, until the shallots soften, about 3 minutes. Add the clam juice mixture with the rice, tomato paste, thyme, and bay leaf. Bring to a boil. Reduce the heat to medium-low and partially cover. Simmer until the rice is very tender, about 25 minutes. Remove the bay leaf.

6. Meanwhile, heat the remaining tablespoon of butter in a medium skillet over medium heat. Add the reserved diced fennel and cook, stirring occasionally, until crisp-tender, about 5 minutes. Season with salt and pepper to taste. Remove from the heat and cover to keep warm.

7. In batches, puree the bisque mixture in a blender. Return the bisque to the saucepan. Add the cream and shelled mussels, and heat just until piping hot; do not boil. Season with salt and pepper.

8. Ladle the bisque into individual soup bowls. Add a spoonful of sautéed fennel to each and sprinkle with fennel fronds or parsley. Serve hot.

Lime and Cilantro Slaw

It is ironic that citrus, which invokes thoughts of sunny places, should be at the peak of its season during the winter months. On the other hand, cabbage, also a winter staple, is likely to remind one of cold climes. Nonetheless, the two complement each other well in this bright-flavored slaw. You might want to serve it with the Soft Tacos with Chipotle Carnitas (page 88).

Grated zest of 1 lime

⅓ cup freshly squeezed lime juice

1 garlic clove, crushed through a press

¾ cup pure olive oil

One 2¼-pound head green cabbage, shredded

6 scallions, white and green parts, chopped

¼ cup finely chopped cilantro

Salt and freshly ground black pepper

1. Whisk the lime zest, lime juice, and garlic together in a large bowl. Gradually whisk in the oil.

2. Add the cabbage, scallions, and cilantro, and mix. Season with salt and pepper to taste. Cover and refrigerate until chilled, at least 2 hours. (The slaw can be made up to 2 days ahead.) Serve chilled.

Roasted Beet and Orange Salad

With its Day-Glo colors, this salad has lots of visual appeal that is more than matched by its mouth-filling flavors. There is no better way to prepare beets than roasting, and I wish I had a nickel for all of the times I've served this to a guest who's said, "I don't even like beets, but I love this salad."

6 medium beets, scrubbed but unpeeled

2 large navel oranges

1 tablespoon balsamic vinegar

⅓ cup extra-virgin olive oil

Salt and freshly ground black pepper

½ small red onion, cut into thin half-moons

1. Position a rack in the center of the oven and preheat to 400°F.

2. To roast the beets, wrap each beet in aluminum foil. Place on a rimmed baking sheet and bake until tender, about 1 hour. Cool completely. Slip the skins off the beets. Slice the beets into thick rounds.

3. To prepare the oranges, grate the zest from half an orange into a medium bowl and set aside. Cut about ½ inch from the top and bottom of each orange and stand them on the work surface. Using a serrated knife, cut off the peel where it meets

the flesh. Working over a small bowl, cut between the membranes to release the orange segments into the bowl. Squeeze the membranes over the bowl to extract any remaining juice. Measure 2 tablespoons of the orange juice into the bowl with the zest.

4. Whisk together the orange zest, juice, and the balsamic vinegar. Gradually whisk in the oil. Season with salt and pepper to taste, and whisk again to dissolve the salt. Add the beets, orange segments, and red onion, and toss gently. Serve at room temperature.

Beets

According to a very unscientific study, performed when creating menus and asking prospective dinner guests if they have any aversions, I have found the most unpopular vegetable: beets. Were the opinions formed during childhood, when forced to eat boring canned beets? Or was it a child's basic mistrust of all vegetables—especially ones that have an unfamiliar hue?

Beets deserve to be loved for their very uniqueness. Most beets are magenta (but there are striped and yellow ones, too, although I mainly see those in the summer), and they can really brighten up a winter table. Roast them (boiling and steaming drains them of flavor and color) and you'll be treated to a combination of earthy and sweet flavors. Their juices, made deep red by the pigment betalain, stain like crazy. You'll release fewer juices if you cut them after cooking. Beet skin is thicker and composed differently than the flesh, so it will slip off easily. There really isn't a good way to remove beet stains, so if it is a concern, wear latex gloves when handling.

If you can, buy beets with the greens still attached, as the perkiness of the leaves indicates freshness. When trimming off the leaves, or any remaining roots at the tip of the beets, don't trim them flush, and leave an inch or two attached, as this will help staunch the flow of the juices.

Poached Leeks with Creamy Vinaigrette

Makes 4 to 6 servings

One January, I found myself in Paris. One of the many pleasures of that trip (and I can assure you that Paris is just as magical when you are sniffling from the cold as when it is warm) was enjoying leeks vinaigrette at a bistro. Simmer the leeks and they'll hold their slender shape beautifully. The vinaigrette, with a soupçon of crème fraîche, is the perfect counterpoint to the silky leeks.

12 medium leeks

3 tablespoons fresh lemon juice

2 tablespoons crème fraîche or sour cream

⅔ cup pure olive oil

Salt and freshly ground black pepper

2 tablespoons finely chopped fresh chives

1. Working with one leek at a time, cut off the dark green top, leaving the white and pale green part intact. Starting about ¼ inch from the root end, slice the leek lengthwise. Rinse well under cold running water, letting the water run between the layers to remove any grit. Transfer to a large bowl of cold water and soak for 10 minutes. Lift the leeks from the water and shake off the excess water.

2. Arrange the leeks, overlapping if necessary, in a large skillet. Add enough lightly salted water to cover. Bring to a simmer over medium heat. Reduce the heat to medium-low and cover. Simmer gently until the leeks are tender, about 20 minutes. They should hold their shape; do not overcook.

3. Using a slotted spoon, carefully transfer the leeks to a platter and let cool. One at a time, gently squeeze the excess water from the leeks and give them a uniform shape. Return the leeks to the platter. Cover and refrigerate until chilled, for at least 1 and up to 12 hours.

4. Whisk the lemon juice and crème fraîche together in a small bowl. Gradually whisk in the oil. Season with salt and pepper to taste, and whisk again to dissolve the salt. Pour over the chilled leeks, sprinkle with the chives, and serve.

MAIN COURSES

Roast Chicken with Radicchio, Currant, and Hazelnut Salad

Roasted Salmon on Spicy Lentils

Cod with Grapefruit, Avocado, and Fennel Salad

San Francisco Crab Cioppino

Cracked Crab with Green Goddess Dip

Rib Roast with Blue Cheese Crust

Roast Eye of Round with Dijon-Caper Sauce

Braised Short Ribs with Dark Beer and Root Vegetables

Sauerbraten

Cider-Brined Roast Pork with Sweet Potatoes and Apples

Baked Ham with Cranberry-Tangerine Glaze

Wine-Braised Sauerkraut and Sausages

Soft Tacos with Chipotle Carnitas

Spanish Panini with Manchego, Jamón Serrano, and Dates

Lamb Shanks with Feta and Olives

Black Bean Chili in Roasted Acorn Squash

Winter Squash Waffles with Maple-Apple Compote

Roast Chicken with Radicchio, Currant, and Hazelnut Salad

Makes 6 servings

The perfect roast chicken has crisp, golden brown skin, juicy flesh, and, in my opinion, very few auxiliary flavors to detract from the chicken itself. Over the years, I have unearthed a few secrets that will help create an irresistible bird, which I have collected and listed in "Tips for a Perfect Roast Chicken" on page 56. In this dish, a vinaigrette is created from the pan juices, which, in turn, is used to dress pleasantly bitter radicchio leaves that are toned down with sweet dried currants. The heat from the dressing and the chicken will lightly wilt the radicchio, which will mellow its flavor even more.

One 6- to 6½-pound chicken

1½ teaspoons kosher salt

½ teaspoon freshly ground black pepper

½ cup plus 1 tablespoon extra-virgin olive oil, divided

2 tablespoons finely minced shallots

2 tablespoons balsamic vinegar

2 heads radicchio, cored and torn into bite-size pieces

½ cup (2 ounces) hazelnuts, toasted, skinned, and coarsely chopped

⅓ cup dried currants

1. Pull the pads of yellow fat from either side of the tail of the chicken. Rinse the chicken and pat dry with paper towels. Let stand at room temperature for 1 to 2 hours.

2. Meanwhile, coarsely chop the fat and place in a small saucepan. Cook over medium-low heat, stirring occasionally, until the fat is rendered and only crisp cracklings

remain in the pan, about 20 minutes. Strain into a small bowl, discarding the cracklings, and cool the fat. You should have 2 to 3 tablespoons of rendered fat.

3. Position a rack in the lower third of the oven and preheat the oven to 425°F. Rub the fat all over the chicken. Season the chicken inside and out with the salt and pepper. Place the chicken on its side on a wire rack in a roasting pan. Roast for 20 minutes. Inserting a wooden spoon in the body cavity, turn the chicken on its other side and roast for 20 minutes more. Turn the chicken breast side up and roast until an instant-read thermometer inserted in the thickest part of the thigh, without touching a bone, reads 170°F, about 1 hour longer. Transfer the chicken to a carving board and let stand for 20 minutes before carving. Remove the rack from the pan.

4. Pour the drippings from the pan into a small glass bowl and let stand for 3 minutes. Skim off and discard the clear yellow fat and reserve the brown pan juices. Add 1 tablespoon of the olive oil to the pan and heat over medium heat. Add the shallots and cook, stirring often, until softened, about 1 minute. Add the vinegar and then the remaining ½ cup olive oil. Whisk until well combined, scraping up the browned bits in the bottom of the pan. Remove from the heat.

5. Combine the radicchio, hazelnuts, and currants in a large bowl. Add the warm dressing and toss. Season the salad with salt and pepper. Transfer the salad to a large platter.

6. Carve the chicken. Arrange the chicken over the radicchio salad, and season the chicken lightly with salt and pepper. Serve at once.

Note
To toast and peel hazelnuts, spread the hazelnuts on a rimmed baking sheet. Bake in a preheated 350°F oven until the skins are cracked and the flesh under the skin is beginning to brown, about 12 minutes. Wrap the nuts in a coarse-textured towel and let cool until easy to handle. Rub the nuts in the towel to remove as much skin as possible (you don't need to remove every bit).

TIPS FOR A PERFECT ROAST CHICKEN ❄

- Roast a large bird in order to have leftovers for another meal. Think beyond a cold drumstick for lunch, and consider turning the meat into a salad or casserole.
- Don't discard the carcass from the roast chicken. It can be made into an excellent stock. Saute ¼ cup each chopped onion, celery, and carrot in 1 tablespoon vegetable oil in a large saucepan. Add the carcass, broken up into manageable pieces, and add enough cold water to cover. (If your chicken came with giblets, reserve the neck, heart, and gizzard—but not the liver—and add them to the pot.) Bring to a simmer, skim off any foam from the surface, and add ¼ teaspoon dried thyme and ½ bay leaf. Simmer for a couple of hours, then strain.
- The chicken will roast more evenly if allowed to stand at room temperature for an hour or two to lose its chill from the refrigerator. A rinse under lukewarm water will also gently warm up the poultry.
- Rendered chicken fat promotes a beautifully browned bird. If the fat has been removed from the tail area of your chicken, substitute 2 tablespoons of softened unsalted butter for the

rendered fat. The milk solids in the butter will encourage browning better than olive or vegetable oil.

- Turning the bird to expose the skin on all sides to the oven heat also makes a picture-perfect chicken with crackling skin. If you don't have time to do this, you'll still have delicious chicken, even if the back skin is a little wan.
- Don't be afraid of the relatively high oven temperature. It will make the chicken splatter, but cleaning the oven is worth the trade-off for a great chicken. You won't get the same results if you chicken out and reduce the temperature to 350°F.

Roasted Salmon on Spicy Lentils

Makes 4 servings

Rich salmon can hold its own against bold seasonings. Here, roasted fillets are served on lentils with a blend of southwestern spices. Roasting lightly caramelizes the top of the salmon to deepen the flavor. Small, dark olive green *lentilles de Puy* have a brighter color than the typical brown lentils, and cook in less time, too. You find them at natural food stores and gourmet shops.

SPICY LENTILS

1 tablespoon extra-virgin olive oil

1 small onion, chopped

½ cup seeded and finely diced red bell pepper

1 garlic clove, minced

1 teaspoon chili powder

½ teaspoon ground cumin

½ teaspoon ground coriander

1 cup green French lentils (*lentilles de Puy*), rinsed and sorted over for stones

2 cups chicken stock, preferably homemade, or use canned low-sodium broth

½ teaspoon salt

1 tablespoon extra-virgin olive oil, plus more for the baking sheet

1½ pounds center-cut salmon fillet with skin

Salt and freshly ground black pepper

1. To make the lentils, heat the oil in a medium saucepan over medium heat. Add the onion and bell pepper and cook, stirring occasionally, until softened, about 3 minutes.

Add the garlic and cook until it is fragrant, about 1 minute. Add the chili powder, cumin, and coriander, and stir until fragrant, about 1 minute. Stir in the lentils, then the stock. Bring to a boil. Reduce the heat to medium-low and cover. Simmer until the lentils are tender, about 30 minutes. During the last 5 minutes, stir in the salt.

2. Meanwhile, position a rack in the center of the oven and preheat the oven to 400°F. Lightly oil a large rimmed baking sheet.

3. Lightly oil the salmon flesh and season with salt and pepper. Place the salmon on the baking sheet, skin side down. Cut the salmon vertically into 4 serving portions, but do not separate the pieces. Roast until the salmon shows the barest sign of pink when pierced in the thickest part with the tip of a knife, about 10 minutes.

4. Divide the lentils evenly among 4 soup bowls. Top each with a portion of the salmon, and serve hot.

Cod with Grapefruit, Avocado, and Fennel Salad

Makes 4 servings

This light and refreshing dish puts me in mind of long weekends in Florida or some other tropical paradise. It takes just a few minutes to prepare, but the mélange of colors and textures is restaurant-worthy. Other mild, firm-fleshed fish fillets, such as red snapper or tilapia, can stand in for the cod.

GRAPEFRUIT, AVOCADO, AND FENNEL SALAD

1 small fennel bulb, preferably with fronds attached

1 tablespoon fresh lemon juice

¼ cup olive oil

Salt and freshly ground black pepper

1 ripe avocado, pitted, peeled, and cut into ½-inch dice

1 pink or red grapefruit, peel removed, cut between the membranes into segments

Four 5- to 6-ounce portions cod fillet

Salt and freshly ground black pepper

2 teaspoons olive oil

1. To prepare the salad, cut the fennel in half lengthwise. If the fronds are attached, cut them off and reserve. Cut out and discard the triangular core at the base of the bulb. Cut one fennel half crosswise into thin half-moons. Reserve the remaining fennel half and stalks for another use.

2. Whisk the lemon juice and oil together in a medium bowl until combined. Season with salt and pepper to taste. Add the fennel, avocado, and grapefruit, and mix gently. Set aside while preparing the cod.

3. Season the cod with salt and pepper. Heat the oil in a large nonstick skillet over medium heat. Add the cod and cover. Cook until the undersides are golden, about 3 minutes. Turn and cook, uncovered, adjusting the heat as needed, until the other side is golden brown and the cod looks barely opaque when flaked in the center with the tip of a knife, about 3 minutes more. Meanwhile, chop enough of the reserved fronds to measure 2 teaspoons.

4. Place a fish fillet and a portion of the salad on each of 4 dinner plates, sprinkle with the chopped fronds, if using, and serve immediately.

San Francisco Crab Cioppino

Makes 6 servings

Cioppino, the Mediterranean-inspired but purely Californian shellfish stew, is one of the best ways to savor the winter's Dungeness crab. I have many happy memories of cooking up a pot of cioppino in my flat in San Francisco, with its fragrant steam fogging up the kitchen windows. As an experienced cioppino cook and eater, I can tell you that it is as messy to eat as it is delicious. Serve it in large, wide bowls with big napkins (or bibs), nutcrackers, and long-stemmed shellfish forks to get the meat out of the shells, a bowl to collect said shells, and bowls of hot lemon water for cleaning your fingers. And don't forget crusty sourdough bread!

3 tablespoons olive oil

1 medium onion, chopped

1 green bell pepper, cored, seeded, and diced

1¼ cups chopped fresh fennel

4 garlic cloves, chopped

1½ cups dry white wine, such as Pinot Grigio

One 28-ounce can crushed tomatoes in puree

One 8-ounce can tomato sauce

2 cups bottled clam juice

1 teaspoon dried oregano

1 teaspoon dried basil

½ teaspoon fennel seed

¼ teaspoon crushed hot red pepper flakes, or more to taste

Salt

3 cooked and cracked Dungeness crabs (see Cracked Crab with
Green Goddess Dip, page 66), about 2 pounds each

Chopped fresh parsley, for garnish

1. Heat the oil in a large pot over medium heat. Add the onion, bell pepper, and fennel. Cover and cook, stirring occasionally, until the vegetables are tender, about 7 minutes. Add the garlic and cook until fragrant, about 2 minutes. Add the wine and increase the heat to high. Boil until the wine is slightly reduced, about 3 minutes.

2. Add the tomatoes and their puree, the tomato sauce, clam juice, oregano, basil, fennel seed, and red pepper flakes. Bring to a boil, stirring often. Reduce the heat to low and simmer, uncovered, stirring occasionally, until lightly thickened, about 1 hour. Season with salt to taste and more pepper flakes, if you wish.

3. Add the cracked crab to the pot and cover. Cook just until the until the crab is heated through, about 3 minutes.

4. Using a ladle and tongs, transfer the cioppino to deep soup bowls. Sprinkle with parsley and serve hot. Tell your guests that it is perfectly fine (if not imperative) to pick up the crab with their fingers.

Variation

Crabmeat Cioppino: I admit that eating classic crab cioppino in the shell is a little sloppy. For a more elegant presentation, substitute shelled crabmeat for the cracked crab. If using fresh crab, remove the crabmeat from the three cooked crabs, and stir the shelled crabmeat into the cioppino broth. Or use 1 pound of cooked lump crabmeat (preferably not pasteurized), picked over for shells and cartilage.

Cracked Crab with Green Goddess Dip

Makes 4 servings

One of the best meals I ever had was at a prewedding dinner for my friends Roseanne and George Dobbins. It was in San Francisco, and all we ate was a mountain of sweet, cracked Dungeness crab with this dip, sourdough bread, and a modest green salad, downed with bottles of Chardonnay. Live Dungeness crabs used to be available only on the West Coast during their winter season, but they are now sold all over the country at many supermarkets and Asian grocers. While you can easily buy freshly cooked and cracked crab from Seattle to San Diego, outside of that region, you may have to cook the crabs yourself. Here's how, and it is the method to use if you are making the cioppino on page 64.

GREEN GODDESS DIP

Grated zest of 1 lemon

2 tablespoons fresh lemon juice

1 teaspoon anchovy paste

1½ cups mayonnaise

3 tablespoons nonpareil capers, drained and rinsed

2 tablespoons finely chopped fresh parsley

2 tablespoons finely chopped fresh chives

1 tablespoon finely chopped fresh tarragon

Freshly ground black pepper

4 live Dungeness crabs, about 2 pounds each

1. To make the dip, whisk together the lemon zest and juice with the anchovy paste in a medium bowl to dissolve the anchovy paste. Add the mayonnaise, capers, parsley, chives, and tarragon. Season with pepper to taste. Stir well. Cover and refrigerate for at least 2 hours. (The dip can be made up to 3 days ahead.)

2. Bring a very large pot of salted water to a rolling boil over high heat. Using tongs, add 1 crab to the pot and cover. Cook for 3 minutes, then set the lid ajar. Continue cooking until the crab is deep red-orange, about 20 minutes (or about 15 minutes for smaller crabs). Using tongs, transfer the crab to a large bowl of cold water, and let stand until easy to handle. Repeat with the remaining crabs, adding more boiling water to the pot as needed. (See Note.)

3. To clean and crack the crabs, work with 1 crab at a time. Turn the crab upside down. Locate and pull off the small triangular "apron" in the lower center of the crab. Pull off the small flippers at the front of the crab. Pull off the top shell in one piece, discarding the shell and any liquid in it. Discard the reddish membrane and any viscera in the body. (Some people save the yellow "fat," but there isn't much and it isn't worth it, in my opinion.) Rinse the body under cold running water. Remove the legs and claws. Using a flat meat cleaver, crack the shells of the legs and claws. Using a heavy knife, cut the body into quarters. Transfer all of the crab pieces to a large bowl. Cover and refrigerate until chilled, at least 1 and up to 12 hours.

4. Serve chilled, with nutcrackers, shellfish forks, and bowls for the shells, as well as individual bowls of the dip.

Note

Even if you have a huge pot, it is most efficient to cook the crabs one at a time. The water should be boiling furiously when the crab is added, which will hasten its final dispatching. Two pots of water will speed things up.

Rib Roast with Blue Cheese Crust

Makes 6 servings

To many cooks, a large, impressive rib roast is the main course of choice for a winter holiday feast. No matter how many other options present themselves, I usually fall back on good old rib roast myself. In an effort to make it different than the straightforward version I've offered in the past, here is a glorious roast with a delicious crust to accent the lush meat. I like this roast just as it is, but you can serve a sauceboat of homemade beef stock alongside to make it "au jus."

One 3½-pound rib roast

1½ teaspoons kosher salt

½ teaspoon freshly ground black pepper

1 tablespoon Dijon mustard

⅔ cup fresh bread crumbs

½ cup (2 ounces) crumbled blue cheese (see Note)

1. Trim excess fat from the surface of the roast. Season the roast all over with the salt and pepper. Let the roast stand at room temperature for at least 1 and up to 2 hours.

2. Position a rack in the center of the oven and preheat the oven to 450°F. Stand the roast, bone side down, in a roasting pan. Roast for 15 minutes. Reduce the oven temperature to 350°F. Continue roasting for 1 hour more.

3. Remove the roast in the pan from the oven. Spread the mustard over the top of the roast. Mix the bread crumbs and blue cheese together in a small bowl. Press the crumb mixture in a layer over the mustard. Return to the oven and roast until the

crust is golden brown and an instant-read thermometer inserted in the center of the meat registers 130°F for medium-rare meat. (If the crust has browned before the roast is cooked to the desired temperature, tent the roast with aluminum foil.)

4. Carefully transfer the roast to a carving board and let stand for 15 to 20 minutes. Carve the roast and serve hot.

Note

For a truly luxurious version, use Roquefort cheese. However, I have used less expensive Maytag Blue and Danish Blue with great success.

Roast Eye of Round with Dijon-Caper Sauce

Makes 6 servings

If there isn't room in the budget for prime rib, don't give up on roast beef. There are other flavorful, and less expensive, cuts of beef, too. For the best results, eye of round should be cooked no more than medium-rare, and sliced thin. Serve it with the Root Vegetables Anna (page 128) and a simple green vegetable, such as steamed green beans.

ROAST BEEF

One 3-pound eye of round beef roast

Salt

1 tablespoon vegetable oil

1 teaspoon dried thyme

1 teaspoon dried basil

½ teaspoon freshly ground black pepper

DIJON-CAPER SAUCE

1 tablespoon unsalted butter

1 tablespoon all-purpose flour

2 cups beef stock, preferably homemade, or use canned low-sodium broth

2 tablespoons Dijon mustard

2 tablespoons nonpareil capers, drained and rinsed

1. To prepare the beef, trim off extraneous fat and sinew. Season all over with salt. Let stand at room temperature for 1 hour before roasting.

2. Position a rack in the center of the oven and preheat to 350°F. Heat the oil in a large skillet over medium-high heat. Add the beef and cook, turning occasionally, until browned on all sides, about 8 minutes. Transfer to a carving board. Mix the thyme, basil, and pepper together in a small bowl. Sprinkle the herb mixture all over the beef. Transfer the beef to a roasting rack in a roasting pan.

3. Roast until an instant-read thermometer inserted in the center of the roast reads 130°F, about 45 minutes. Transfer the beef to a carving board. Let stand about 15 minutes while making the sauce.

4. To make the sauce, place the roasting pan over medium heat. Add the butter to the pan drippings in the pan and melt. Add the flour and whisk until smooth. Whisk in the stock and bring to a boil. Cook, whisking often, until reduced to 1¼ cups, about 6 minutes. Whisk in the mustard and capers. Season with salt and pepper. Transfer to a sauceboat.

5. Carve the beef into thin slices and serve hot with the sauce.

Braised Short Ribs with Dark Beer and Root Vegetables

Makes 6 servings

It really breaks my heart to see boneless cuts of meat taking over the butcher case at the market. Every good cook knows that stews made with bone-in cuts give flavor to the braising liquid, and also add body as they give off their gelatin into the simmering sauce. Here is a fine braise, chock-full of meaty short ribs (look for the ones that are cut into individual bones, and not the cross-cut flanken) and earthy root vegetables. Make plenty of mashed potatoes to serve alongside.

3 tablespoons vegetable oil, divided

5 pounds short ribs, cut into 3-inch lengths

2 teaspoons salt

½ teaspoon freshly ground black pepper

3 medium carrots, 1 finely chopped and 2 cut into 1-inch chunks

1 small celery rib with leaves, finely chopped

½ cup coarsely chopped shallots

8 tablespoons (1 stick) unsalted butter

½ cup all-purpose flour

Two 12-ounce bottles dark beer

2 cups beef stock, preferably homemade, or use canned low-sodium broth

2 tablespoons dark brown sugar

1 tablespoon Dijon mustard

1 tablespoon tomato paste

1 teaspoon dried thyme

1 bay leaf

2 medium parsnips, cut into 1-inch chunks

2 large red-skinned potatoes, unpeeled, cut into 1-inch chunks

Chopped fresh parsley, for garnish

1. Position a rack in the center of the oven and preheat to 300°F.

2. Heat 2 tablespoons of the oil in a very large Dutch oven over medium-high heat. Season the short ribs with the salt and pepper. In batches, add the short ribs to the Dutch oven and cook, turning occasionally, until browned on all sides, about 5 minutes. Transfer to a platter.

3. Add the remaining 1 tablespoon oil to the Dutch oven. Add the finely chopped carrot and celery, and reduce the heat to medium. Cook, stirring up the browned bits in the Dutch oven with a wooden spatula, until softened, about 3 minutes. Add the shallots and cook until they soften, about 2 minutes.

4. Add the butter and melt. Sprinkle in the flour and let bubble for 1 minute. Whisk in the beer, then the stock, brown sugar, mustard, tomato paste, thyme, and bay leaf. Bring to a boil over high heat. Return the short ribs to the Dutch oven, meaty sides down.

5. Cover and bake for 2 hours. Remove from the oven and stir in the parsnips, potatoes, and remaining carrots. Return to the oven and continue baking until the vegetables are tender, about 45 minutes longer. Skim off any fat on the surface, and serve hot, garnished with the parsley.

Sauerbraten

My cousin Judy and I love to swap recipes, especially those that remind us of our family's Austrian (actually Liechtensteiner!) heritage. She asked if I had a good recipe for the marinated spiced pot roast sauerbraten, and by coincidence, I had just developed this recipe a few days before. The trick for using balsamic vinegar comes from my German-born friend Erna Zahn, and as far as cooking is concerned, what she says goes. Remember: the beef needs to marinate for at least 2 days before braising. And, if you're going to make sauerbraten, you may as well serve Mom's Red Cabbage (page 133) and Homemade Spaetzle with Herb Butter (page 116), too.

MARINADE

1½ cups hearty red wine, such as Shiraz

1 cup red wine vinegar

2 medium yellow onions, chopped

2 medium carrots, chopped

2 celery ribs, chopped

4 quarter-sized slices fresh ginger

1 teaspoon allspice berries

½ teaspoon whole cloves

½ teaspoon black peppercorns

½ teaspoon yellow mustard seed

One 3-inch cinnamon stick

3 bay leaves

One 3-pound beef rump roast

1 teaspoon salt

½ teaspoon freshly ground black pepper

3 bacon strips, coarsely chopped

1 tablespoon vegetable oil, plus more as needed

1 medium onion, chopped

1 medium carrot, chopped

1 celery rib, chopped

2 cups beef stock, preferably homemade, or use low-sodium canned broth

½ cup crushed gingersnap cookies

2 tablespoons balsamic vinegar

Salt and freshly ground black pepper

1. At least 3 days before cooking, make the marinade. Mix all of the ingredients with 1 cup water in a large, deep, nonreactive bowl. Add the rump roast and cover. Refrigerate, turning occasionally in the marinade, for at least 2 and up to 3 days.

2. Remove the meat from the marinade and pat it dry with paper towels. Season with the salt and pepper. Strain the marinade and reserve 2 cups.

3. Position a rack in the center of the oven and preheat to 325°F.

4. Cook the bacon and oil in a large Dutch oven over medium-high heat until the bacon is crisp and browned. Using a slotted spoon, transfer the bacon to paper towels to drain. Pour the fat into a small heatproof bowl.

5. Return 2 tablespoons of the fat to the Dutch oven and heat over medium-high heat. Add the beef and cook, turning occasionally, until browned on all sides, about 8 minutes, adding more vegetable oil as needed. Transfer to a plate.

6. Add the remaining bacon fat to the Dutch oven and reduce the heat to medium. Add the onion, carrot, and celery and cook, stirring occasionally, until softened, about 5 minutes. Add the reserved marinade and stock, and bring to a boil over high heat. Add the beef and reserved bacon, and return to the boil.

7. Cover tightly and bake, turning the meat occasionally in the liquid, until fork-tender, about 3½ hours. Transfer the meat to a platter and tent with aluminum foil to keep warm.

8. Skim off the fat from the surface of the cooking liquid. Place the pot over high heat and bring to a boil. Cook until reduced to about 2 cups, about 10 minutes. Whisk in the gingersnaps and cook until lightly thickened, about 3 minutes. Stir in the balsamic vinegar and season with salt and pepper to taste.

9. Slice the sauerbraten across the grain. Spoon the sauce on top and serve hot.

Cider-Brined Roast Pork with Sweet Potatoes and Apples

Makes 6 to 8 servings

This one-pot meal will fill your kitchen with the appetite-arousing meaty aroma of roasting pork and the fragrance of caramelizing root vegetables. If you can, use white-fleshed "true" sweet potatoes instead of orange-fleshed yams for this dish. Sautéed kale would be perfect on the side.

BRINE

Two 12-ounce bottles hard apple or pear cider

½ cup table salt

¼ cup packed light brown sugar

1 tablespoon dried rosemary

1 tablespoon dried sage

1 tablespoon dried thyme

1 teaspoon fennel seed

1 teaspoon black peppercorns

2 bay leaves

4½ cups ice water

One 4-pound center-cut pork loin with bones (6 ribs)

2 white-fleshed sweet potatoes, peeled and cut into 1-inch chunks

2 Golden Delicious apples, peeled, cored, and cut lengthwise into sixths

1 tablespoon vegetable oil

Salt and freshly ground black pepper

1 teaspoon finely chopped fresh rosemary

1. To make the brine, about 8 hours before roasting the pork, bring the cider, salt, brown sugar, rosemary, sage, thyme, fennel seed, peppercorns, and bay leaves to a simmer in a medium nonreactive saucepan over medium heat, stirring often to dissolve the salt. Transfer to a large deep bowl and let cool until tepid. Add the ice water and stir well. Add the pork to the brine. Cover and refrigerate, turning the pork occasionally in the brine, for at least 4 and up to 6 hours, but no longer.

2. Position a rack in the center of the oven and preheat to 450°F.

3. Drain the pork and pat it dry with paper towels. Place the pork in a roasting pan, meaty side up. Roast for 45 minutes.

4. Toss the sweet potatoes and apples together with the vegetable oil in a large bowl. Season with salt and pepper. Spread around the pork and stir with the juices in the pan to coat. Continue roasting until an instant-read thermometer inserted in the center of the roast reads 140°F, about 40 minutes more. Transfer the pork to a platter and tent it with aluminum foil. Let stand for 10 to 20 minutes while roasting the sweet potatoes and apples.

5. Stir the sweet potatoes and apples and continue roasting until they are tender, about 10 minutes. Using a slotted spoon, transfer them to a serving bowl, sprinkle with the rosemary, and toss gently. Scatter around the pork on the platter and cover again with foil to keep warm while making the sauce.

6. Leaving any browned bits in the pan, pour out the fat. Place the pan over medium heat. Add the butter and let melt. Whisk in the flour and let bubble until very lightly browned, about 2 minutes. Whisk in the cider, then the stock, and bring to a simmer. Reduce the heat to medium-low and simmer until thickened and no taste of raw flour remains, about 3 minutes. Season with salt and pepper to taste. Pour into a sauceboat.

7. Carve the roast and serve hot with the sweet potatoes and apples, and the sauce on the side.

Baked Ham with Cranberry-Tangerine Glaze

Makes about 12 servings

During the festive holiday season, we have ample opportunity to feed a large group, and ham has long been the main course of choice when serving a crowd. Always opt for a ham on the bone, which will be much more flavorful than a presliced one. (The juices lost during the preslicing are replaced with salt water, making these hams too salty for my taste.) This recipe makes double use of a vibrant magenta cranberry-tangerine relish, as some of the juices are used to glaze the ham, while the remainder is served alongside.

CRANBERRY-TANGERINE RELISH

9 tangerines

One 12-ounce bag cranberries, rinsed and sorted

1 cup sugar

One 6½-pound smoked ham half on the bone

12 ounces ginger ale

1. To make the glaze, grate the zest from 2 tangerines and reserve. Cut 7 of the tangerines in half crosswise and squeeze the juice from them. You should have 1 cup tangerine juice. Peel the remaining 2 tangerines and separate them into segments. Cut each segment in half crosswise, discarding any seeds. Set the chopped tangerines aside.

2. Combine the cranberries, tangerine juice and zest, and sugar together in a large saucepan. Cook over medium heat just until all of the berries have burst and given off their juices and the juices are boiling. Strain in a wire sieve over a bowl. Measure out and reserve ¾ cup of the juices.

3. Transfer the cranberry mixture and any remaining juices to a medium bowl and let cool. Stir in the reserved chopped tangerines. Cover and refrigerate until chilled, at least 1 hour. (The relish can be made up to 1 day ahead.)

4. Position a rack in the center of the oven and preheat to 350°F. Line a roasting pan with aluminum foil.

5. Trim the exterior fat on the ham to ¼-inch thickness. Score the ham in a crosshatch pattern with ⅛-inch-deep score marks about 1 inch apart. Place the ham on a roasting rack in the pan, flat side down, with the bone sticking up. Pour the ginger ale over the ham. Cover the pan with aluminum foil.

6. Bake for 1½ hours. Discard the foil. Pour the reserved cranberry juice mixture over the ham. Continue baking, occasionally basting with the pan juices, until the ham is glazed and an instant-read thermometer inserted in the thickest part of the ham (but not touching a bone) reads 140°F, about 45 minutes. If the ham gets too brown, tent it with foil. If the glaze threatens to scorch, add water to the pan.

7. Transfer the ham to a platter and let stand 15 minutes. Carve the ham. Pour the pan juices over the sliced ham and serve with the cranberry-tangerine relish on the side.

Wine-Braised Sauerkraut and Sausages

Makes 6 servings

This is a simplified version of *choucroute garni*, a dish I learned to love when I was studying cuisine in Paris, and found myself eating in inexpensive brasseries much more often than Michelin-starred fine restaurants. Who knew that humble sauerkraut could be so delicious? There are two secrets here: refrigerated (not canned) sauerkraut and a fruity (not dry) white wine. While I usually make it with sausages, *c'est magnifique* with smoked pork chops or even a slice of ham.

4 slices bacon, coarsely chopped

2 medium onions, chopped

4 garlic cloves, finely chopped

3 pounds refrigerated sauerkraut, drained well (see Note)

2 cups semidry white wine, such as Riesling or Pinot Blanc

1 cup chicken stock, preferably homemade, or use canned low-sodium broth

6 juniper berries, crushed, or 2 tablespoons gin (optional)

1 bay leaf

1 teaspoon vegetable oil

6 cooked chicken and apple sausages, frankfurters,
    or your favorite cooked sausages, each pierced with a fork

1 pound kielbasa, cut into 6 serving pieces

Dijon or grainy mustard, for serving

1. Position a rack in the center of the oven and preheat to 300°F.

2. Cook the bacon in a Dutch oven over medium heat, stirring occasionally, until crisp and browned, about 8 minutes. Using a slotted spoon, transfer to paper towels to drain, leaving the fat in the Dutch oven.

3. Add the onions and cook, stirring occasionally, until tender, about 5 minutes. Stir in the garlic and cook until it gives off its fragrance, about 1 minute. Stir in the sauerkraut, wine, stock, juniper berries (if using), and bay leaf, and bring to a boil. Cover and bake for 45 minutes.

4. Heat the oil in a large skillet over medium heat. Add the sausages and cook, turning occasionally, until lightly browned, about 3 minutes. Transfer to a plate. Lightly brown the kielbasa in the same skillet, and bury it in the sauerkraut. Continue baking, uncovered, until the sausages are heated through, about 20 minutes. Remove the bay leaf.

5. Using a slotted spoon, serve hot from the Dutch oven, with the mustard on the side.

Note

Refrigerated sauerkraut, packed in plastic bags, can be found near the frankfurters at the supermarket. If you prefer less tangy sauerkraut, rinse it under cold running water, then drain well.

Soft Tacos with Chipotle Carnitas

Makes 6 servings

Pork shoulder is one of the great meat cuts. Sure, it takes a long time to cook, but the flavorful reward is worth the time. Here, I've cooked chunks of it the Mexican way, simmered until they are fall-apart tender, and stuffed them into hot tortillas to make soft tacos. This recipe doesn't depend on garden-fresh ingredients to be delicious, making it perfect winter fare.

CARNITAS

3 tablespoons olive oil, divided

3 pounds boneless pork shoulder, cut into 1-inch chunks

½ teaspoon salt, plus more to taste

½ teaspoon freshly ground black pepper, plus more to taste

1 medium onion, thinly sliced

6 garlic cloves, coarsely chopped

2 teaspoons dried oregano

1 teaspoon ground cumin

2 bay leaves

CHIPOTLE SAUCE

One 15½-ounce can plum tomatoes in juice, drained

1 medium onion, coarsely chopped

2 garlic cloves, finely chopped

2 canned chipotle chiles in adobo, chopped, to taste

1 tablespoon olive oil

1 tablespoon cider vinegar

Corn tortillas, for serving

1. To make the carnitas, position a rack in the center of the oven and preheat to 300°F.

2. Heat 2 tablespoons of the oil in a Dutch oven over medium-high heat. Season the pork with the $\frac{1}{2}$ teaspoons of the salt and pepper. In batches, add the pork to the Dutch oven and cook, stirring occasionally, until lightly browned, about 5 minutes. Using a slotted spoon, transfer the pork to a plate, leaving the fat in the Dutch oven.

3. Add the remaining 1 tablespoon oil to the Dutch oven and reduce the heat to medium. Add the onion and cook, stirring occasionally, until softened, about 3 minutes. Stir in the garlic and cook until it gives off its fragrance, about 1 minute. Pour in 1 cup water and bring to a boil, scraping up the browned bits in the Dutch oven with a wooden spatula.

4. Return the pork to the Dutch oven. Add the oregano, cumin, and bay leaves, and stir well. Cover and bake until the pork is very tender, about 2 hours.

5. Using a slotted spoon, transfer the pork to a platter. Boil the cooking liquid in the Dutch oven until reduced to about $\frac{1}{2}$ cup, about 20 minutes.

6. Meanwhile, make the chipotle sauce. Puree the tomatoes, onion, garlic, and chipotles together in a blender. Heat the oil in a large saucepan over medium heat. Add the puree (it will splatter, so be careful) and bring to a boil. Cook, stirring often, until reduced by about half, about 5 minutes. Stir in the pork and vinegar and cook until the pork is heated through, about 3 minutes. Season with salt and pepper to taste.

7. Transfer to a serving bowl and serve hot with warm tortillas on the side.

Spanish Panini with Manchego, Jamón Serrano, and Dates

Makes 2 sandwiches

This is a grilled cheese sandwich for adults, made with some of the most distinctly flavorful ingredients on the planet. Sharp Manchego plays off the salty Serrano ham, and the sweet, chewy dates have a harmonizing effect. Jamón Serrano is really the best choice here, because other country-style hams, such as prosciutto, may be too salty.

4 slices firm white sandwich bread

6 ounces Manchego, thinly sliced with a sharp knife

4 ounces thinly sliced Jamón Serrano (see Note)

4 Medjool dates, pitted and chopped with a wet knife

3 tablespoons unsalted butter, well softened

1. Place 2 bread slices on the work surface. Top the bread with half of the cheese, then all of the ham. Sprinkle with the dates, then top with the remaining cheese and bread slices.

2. Line a baking sheet with wax paper. Spread the exteriors of both sandwiches with softened butter. Place on the baking sheet. Refrigerate until the butter is firm and the sandwiches release easily from the wax paper, about 30 minutes.

3. Heat a panini pan or ridged iron skillet over medium-high heat. Reduce the heat to medium-low. Place the panini in the pan and weight them with the pan lid or a

heatproof plate. Cook until the undersides of the panini are golden brown, about 5 minutes. Remove the lid and turn the panini. Replace the lid and cook until the other sides are golden brown, about 4 minutes more.

4. Transfer the sandwiches to a chopping board. Cut each sandwich in half and serve hot.

Note

Jamón Serrano, dry-cured Spanish ham, is available sliced to order at many specialty food stores. You may also find a packaged presliced version at a well-stocked supermarket.

Lamb Shanks with Feta and Olives

Meaty lamb shanks are one of my favorite cuts for winter cooking. They are so hearty that it's hard to imagine serving them during warm weather. Nonetheless, the tomatoes and rosemary in this braise gives the dish a sunny Mediterranean feeling. Serve it spooned over orzo, pasta, or rice, or, as my Greek friends do, with roasted potato wedges.

2 tablespoons olive oil, plus more as needed

4 lamb shanks, about 1¼ pounds each

1 teaspoon salt, plus more to taste

½ teaspoon freshly ground black pepper, plus more to taste

1 large onion, chopped

4 garlic cloves, finely chopped

1 cup hearty red wine, such as Shiraz

One 28-ounce can crushed tomatoes in puree

One 15½-ounce can diced tomatoes in juice

1 tablespoon crumbled dried rosemary

½ teaspoon crushed hot red pepper flakes

1 cup pitted and coarsely chopped Kalamata olives

¾ cup (6 ounces) crumbled feta cheese

1. Position a rack in the center of the oven and preheat to 300°F.

2. Heat the oil in a Dutch oven over medium-high heat. Season the lamb shanks with the salt and pepper. In batches, add them to the Dutch oven and cook, turning occasionally, until browned on all sides, about 5 minutes. Transfer to a plate.

3. If needed, add a little more oil to the Dutch oven and heat over medium heat. Add the onion and cook, stirring occasionally, until tender, about 5 minutes. Stir in the garlic and cook until it gives off its fragrance, about 1 minute. Add the wine and bring to a boil, stirring up the browned bits in the Dutch oven with a wooden spatula. Stir in the crushed tomatoes, diced tomatoes with their juice, rosemary, and red pepper flakes. Return the lamb shanks to the Dutch oven and bring to a boil.

4. Cover tightly and bake until the lamb is very tender, about 2½ hours. During the last few minutes, stir in the olives.

5. Season the sauce with salt and pepper to taste. Serve the lamb shanks hot, sprinkled with the feta cheese.

Black Bean Chili in Roasted Acorn Squash

Makes 6 servings

There's nothing like spicy chili to warm you from the inside out. But even when the weather calls for hearty fare, I sometimes prefer something a little lighter than the typical meaty bowl of red. When that happens, I turn to this vegetarian stew. Serving the chili in roasted squash halves looks dramatic, and the sweet squash is a nice accent for the zesty chili.

ACORN SQUASH

Olive oil for the roasting pan and squash

3 acorn squash, about 18 ounces each

Salt and freshly ground black pepper

BLACK BEAN CHILI

2 tablespoons olive oil

1 medium onion, chopped

½ green bell pepper, seeded and ribbed, diced

2 garlic cloves, finely chopped

8 ounces cremini mushrooms, quartered

1 teaspoon ground cumin

1 teaspoon dried oregano

Two 15- to 19-ounce cans black beans, drained and rinsed

One 15½-ounce can diced tomatoes in juice

½ to 1 canned chipotle chile in adobo, finely chopped, to taste

2 tablespoons chopped fresh cilantro

1. Position a rack in the center of the oven and preheat to 400°F. Lightly oil a roasting pan.

2. To prepare the squash, cut each squash in half lengthwise and remove the seeds. Brush the cut surfaces with oil and season with salt and pepper. Place, cut sides down, in the roasting pan. Add ½ cup water and cover with aluminum foil. Bake until tender, about 45 minutes.

3. Meanwhile, make the chili. Heat the oil in a large saucepan over medium heat. Add the onion and green pepper and cook, stirring occasionally, until softened, about 3 minutes. Stir in the garlic. Add the mushrooms and cook, stirring occasionally, until they begin to brown, about 5 minutes. Stir in the cumin and oregano. Stir in the beans and the tomatoes with their juice and bring to a boil. Reduce the heat to medium-low and simmer until the tomato juices thicken, about 20 minutes. Stir in the chipotle, being judicious, and the cilantro. Season with salt and pepper to taste.

4. Place an acorn half, cut side up, in each of 6 bowls. Fill with the chili and serve hot.

Winter Squash Waffles with Maple-Apple Compote

Makes about six 8-inch square waffles

Winter mornings mean digging into a warm breakfast while still in a flannel robe and slippers. I like to serve these waffles as a special treat on Christmas or New Year's Day, when a big breakfast will hold us over until our late-afternoon holiday supper. They are really great with fresh squash, but if you don't have any handy, use canned pumpkin or puree thawed frozen butternut squash in a food processor or blender. Note that waffle irons vary greatly in size, so your yield will vary. My waffle iron makes 8-inch square waffles that are divided into quadrants.

MAPLE-APPLE COMPOTE

2 tablespoons unsalted butter, plus more for serving

2 Golden Delicious or Fuji apples, peeled, cored, and cut into ½-inch dice

1 cup pure maple syrup

WAFFLES

2⅔ cups all-purpose flour

⅓ cup plus 1 tablespoon sugar

4 teaspoons baking powder

½ teaspoon salt

2 cups winter squash puree (see Note)

2 cups whole milk

4 large eggs, separated

6 tablespoons unsalted butter, melted

Cooking oil spray for the waffle iron

1. To make the compote, melt the butter in a large skillet over medium heat. Add the apples and cook, stirring occasionally, until just tender, about 5 minutes. Stir in the syrup and remove from the heat.

2. To make the waffles, preheat a waffle iron according to the manufacturer's instructions. Position a rack in the center of the oven and preheat to 200°F. Line a baking sheet with two clean, fragrance-free kitchen towels (meaning ones that have not been washed with softeners or the like).

3. Whisk the flour, sugar, baking powder, and salt together in a large bowl. Make a well in the center. Whisk the squash puree, milk, egg yolks, and melted butter together in another bowl. Pour into the well and stir just until combined—the mixture will look a little lumpy.

4. Whip the egg whites in another bowl until soft peaks form. Stir one-fourth into the batter to lighten it, then fold in the remaining egg whites.

5. Spray the waffle iron grids with the cooking spray. Add about 1 cup of the batter to the center of the bottom grid and close the waffle iron. Cook until the waffle is golden brown, 3 to 5 minutes. Transfer to the baking sheet, wrap loosely in the towels, and keep warm in the oven while making the remaining waffles.

6. Serve warm, topped with the compote.

Note

To prepare winter squash puree, start by choosing the right squash. Hubbard or butternut are reliably dense and make a firm puree. Cut the unpeeled squash into large chunks (the exact size will depend on the shape of the squash), and remove the seeds and fibers. Place in a roasting pan and add ¼ cup water. Cover with aluminum foil. Bake in a preheated 400°F oven for 30 minutes. Uncover and continue baking until the squash is tender when pierced with a knife, 15 to 30 minutes (depending on the variety of squash). Cool until easy to handle and cut off the peel. Puree the flesh in a food procesor or blender. Transfer to a bowl. To judge the thickness of the puree, stand a wooden spoon in the puree. If it falls over, the puree is too thin. Transfer the puree to a cheesecloth-lined wire sieve placed over a bowl and let drain until the puree is thick enough to support the spoon. The puree can be covered and refrigerated for up to 2 days, or frozen for up to 2 months.

PASTAS

Asian Chicken Salad with Spicy Orange Vinaigrette

Shrimp Jambalaya Ziti

Baked Penne with Farmhouse Cheddar and Leeks

Linguine with Mussels and Sun-Dried Tomatoes

Winter Greens and Walnut Lasagna

Cheese Ravioli with Wild Mushroom and Marsala Sauce

Homemade Spaetzle with Herb Butter

Asian Chicken Salad with Spicy Orange Vinaigrette

Makes 4 to 6 servings

Although winter is the time for rib-sticking food, there are times when a lighter meal would be appropriate—maybe you live someplace where the weather is warm, or you need a refreshing entrée to serve to company for lunch. This salad gives off bursts of flavor; however, it is the familiar but welcome taste of orange that brings it all together.

2 chicken breast halves with skin and bone (about 1 pound total)

Three ¼-inch slices fresh ginger

1 scallion, white and green parts, coarsely chopped

1 teaspoon salt

SPICY ORANGE VINAIGRETTE

2 seedless oranges

2 tablespoons soy sauce

1½ tablespoons unseasoned rice vinegar

2 teaspoons hoisin sauce

1 teaspoon Asian hot sauce, such as sriracha

½ cup vegetable oil

1 tablespoon Asian dark sesame oil

½ pound dried Chinese noodles or linguine

1 cucumber, peeled, halved lengthwise, seeded, and cut into ¼-inch-thick half-moons

2 scallions, white and green parts, thinly sliced

½ red bell pepper, cored, seeded, and cut into thin strips

3 tablespoons chopped fresh cilantro or mint

1. Place the chicken, ginger, scallion, and salt in a saucepan and add enough cold water to cover the chicken. Bring to a boil over high heat. Reduce the heat to low and cover. Simmer until the chicken loses its raw look, about 15 minutes. Remove from the heat and let stand, covered, for 20 minutes. Drain the chicken (the broth can be reserved for Asian recipes). Let the chicken cool until easy to handle. Remove and discard the skin and bone. Pull the chicken meat into shreds.

2. To make the vinaigrette, grate the zest from 1 orange into a small bowl and reserve. Cut off the peel from the oranges. Working over another bowl to collect the juices, cut between the membranes to release the orange segments. Squeeze the juice from the membranes, if necessary, to measure 2 tablespoons.

3. Whisk together the orange juice and zest, soy sauce, vinegar, hoisin sauce, and hot sauce until combined. Gradually whisk in the vegetable oil, then the sesame oil.

4. Bring a large pot of salted water to a boil over high heat. Add the noodles and cook according to the package directions until tender. Drain and rinse under cold running water. Drain well.

5. Transfer the noodles to a bowl. Add the chicken, orange segments, cucumber, scallions, and bell pepper. Add the vinaigrette and toss well. Sprinkle with the cilantro. Taste and season with soy sauce and hot sauce, as desired. Serve at room temperature.

Shrimp Jambalaya Ziti

Makes 6 servings

Mardi Gras is usually celebrated in winter, when it reminds the celebrants that spring will return, just as it does every year. Even if you aren't in New Orleans, this dish celebrates the holiday with Cajun flavors. And consider serving it as the main dish at a Super Bowl party.

2 tablespoons olive oil

8 ounces andouille or kielbasa sausage, cut into ½-inch dice

1 large onion, chopped

1 medium red bell pepper, cored, seeded, and diced

2 medium celery ribs, chopped

3 scallions, chopped

2 garlic cloves, finely chopped

1 teaspoon dried oregano

1 teaspoon dried basil

1 teaspoon sweet paprika, preferably Spanish or Hungarian

⅛ teaspoon cayenne pepper

One 28-ounce can crushed tomatoes with puree

1 pound medium shrimp, peeled and deveined

1 pound ziti, penne, or rigatoni

Freshly grated Parmesan, for serving

1. Heat the oil in a large saucepan over medium heat. Add the andouille and cook, stirring often, until lightly browned, about 5 minutes. Using a slotted spoon, transfer the andouille to a plate, leaving the fat in the saucepan.

2. Add the onion, bell pepper, celery, scallions, and garlic. Cook, stirring occasionally, until softened, about 5 minutes. Add the oregano, basil, paprika, and cayenne, and stir well. Return the andouille to the saucepan. Add the tomatoes and their puree and bring to a boil. Reduce the heat to medium-low and partially cover. Simmer until the puree is lightly thickened, about 45 minutes. During the last 3 minutes, add the shrimp and cook until they turn opaque.

3. Meanwhile, bring a large pot of lightly salted water to a boil over high heat. Add the ziti and cook according to the package instructions until barely tender. Drain well.

4. Return the ziti to the pot. Add the sauce and mix well. Serve hot, with the cheese on the side.

Super Bowl Menu

Sweet and Spicy Chicken Wings (page 5)

Your favorite dips and chips

Shrimp Jambalaya Ziti (opposite)

Garlic bread

Pear and Crystallized Ginger Gingerbread (page 167)

Baked Penne with Farmhouse Cheddar and Leeks

Makes 6 servings

Leeks lift this macaroni and cheese out of the ordinary. If your kids would rebel at leeks in their favorite noodle dish, just leave the leeks out and decrease the mustard to 1 teaspoon. This dish is truly sensational when made with first-class white Cheddar, and when I am feeling really flush, I'll use a British farmhouse cheese.

1 pound penne

4 tablespoons (½ stick) unsalted butter, plus more for the baking dish

4 large leeks, white and pale green parts only, well rinsed, drained, and chopped (5 cups)

¼ cup flour

3½ cups whole milk, heated

4 cups (1 pound) shredded extra-sharp white Cheddar

1 tablespoon Dijon mustard

½ teaspoon hot red pepper sauce

Salt

2 large eggs

1. Preheat the oven to 400°F. Lightly butter a 15 x 10-inch baking dish.

2. Bring a large pot of salted water to a boil over high heat. Add the penne and cook, stirring occasionally, until barely tender (remember the pasta will be baked), about 8 minutes. Drain well.

3. Meanwhile, melt the butter in a large saucepan over medium heat. Add the leeks and cover. Cook, stirring occasionally, until the leeks are tender but not browned, about 10 minutes. Uncover and stir in the flour. Whisk in the milk. Bring to a simmer over medium heat, stirring often. Remove from the heat. Stir in the Cheddar, mustard, and red pepper sauce. Season with salt and additional red pepper sauce to taste.

4. Whisk the eggs in a medium bowl. Gradually whisk in about 1 cup of the hot cheese sauce, then stir the egg and cheese mixture back into the saucepan. Add the penne to the sauce and stir well. Spread in the baking dish.

5. Bake, uncovered, until the sauce is bubbling and the ends of the penne are tinged with brown, about 25 minutes. Serve hot.

Linguine with Mussels and Sun-Dried Tomatoes

Makes 4 to 6 servings

This recipe turns to the pantry and brings the concentrated flavor of sun-dried tomatoes to this wintertime version of the ever-popular linguine with shellfish. Farm-raised mussels won't need to be scrubbed or soaked, but if you have ocean-harvest mussels, use pliers to pull off the "beards," give them a good scrub, then soak in cold salted water for an hour or so to help them expel any grit.

1 pound dried linguine

¼ cup olive oil

2 garlic cloves, finely chopped

½ cup drained and diced oil-packed sun-dried tomatoes

⅔ cup dry white wine

1 teaspoon dried oregano

¼ teaspoon crushed hot red pepper flakes, or more to taste

2 pounds mussels

2 tablespoons unsalted butter, thinly sliced

Salt

Chopped fresh parsley, for garnish

1. Bring a large pot of lightly salted water to a boil over high heat. Add the linguine and cook according to the package directions, stirring occasionally, until al dente.

2. Meanwhile, heat the oil and garlic together in a large pot over medium heat until the garlic is softened but not browned, about 2 minutes. Add the tomatoes, wine, oregano, and red pepper flakes, and increase the heat to high. Add the mussels and cover tightly. Cook, occasionally shaking the pot, until all of the mussels have opened, about 5 minutes. Discard any unopened mussels. Remove from the heat and add the butter. Swirl the pot by its handles until the butter has melted into the sauce. Season the sauce with salt to taste (although it is unlikely to need it because of the saline mussels) and more red pepper flakes, if you wish.

3. Drain the linguine well and transfer to the mussel sauce. Using tongs, add equal amounts of linguine, mussels, and sauce to pasta bowls. Sprinkle with the parsley and serve hot.

Winter Greens and Walnut Lasagna

Makes 12 servings

One of my best friends, Skip, is a vegetarian, and I enjoy coming up with vegetarian dishes that even a carnivore would savor. The idea for this lasagna came to me when I was testing recipes for this book and had a refrigerator full of leafy bitter greens. Like most lasagna dishes, it isn't quick to make, but the return on your time investment is very high.

FILLING

3 pounds assorted winter greens, such as chard, escarole, and kale

2 tablespoons olive oil

1 large onion, chopped

2 garlic cloves, finely chopped

Salt and freshly ground black pepper

3 cups whole-milk ricotta

1 cup toasted (see Note) and coarsely chopped walnuts

½ cup (2 ounces) freshly grated Parmesan

3 large eggs, beaten

3 tablespoons finely chopped fresh parsley

¼ teaspoon freshly grated nutmeg

SAUCE

3 tablespoons unsalted butter

3 tablespoons all-purpose flour

1½ cups whole milk, heated

½ cup (2 ounces) freshly grated Parmesan

Salt and freshly ground black pepper

1 pound dried lasagna

4 cups (1 pound) shredded mozzarella

½ cup (2 ounces) freshly grated Parmesan

2 tablespoons butter, cut into small cubes, plus more for the dish

1. To make the filling, remove the tough stems from the greens. Chop the stems into ½-inch-thick pieces. Fill a sink with cold water and add the stems. Wash the stems well. Lift out of the water and set aside in a bowl; do not dry. Fill the sink with fresh water. A few at a time, stack the leaves and cut crosswise into ½-inch-wide strips. Add to the water and wash well. Lift out of the water and transfer to a large colander; do not dry.

2. Heat the oil in a large saucepan over medium heat. Add the onion and cook, stirring occasionally, until golden, about 5 minutes. Stir in the garlic and cook until fragrant, about 1 minute. Add the stems and cover. Cook until the stems are crisp-tender, about 5 minutes. Stir in the greens, season with salt and pepper, and cover. Cook until the leaves are very tender, about 15 minutes. Drain in a colander and let cool until easy to handle.

3. A handful at a time, squeeze the excess liquid from the greens, and place the greens in a large bowl. Add the ricotta, walnuts, Parmesan, eggs, parsley, 1½ teaspoons salt, ½ teaspoon pepper, and the nutmeg. Mix well.

4. To make the sauce, melt the butter in a medium saucepan over medium-low heat. Whisk in the flour and let the roux bubble without browning for 1 minute. Whisk in

the hot milk and increase the heat to medium. Cook, whisking often, until the sauce is boiling and thickened. Remove from the heat. Stir in the Parmesan and season with salt and pepper to taste. Cover and set aside.

5. Meanwhile, bring a large pot of salted water to a boil over high heat. Stir in the lasagna and cook according to the package directions until al dente. Drain and rinse under cold running water.

6. Lightly butter a 13 x 9-inch baking dish. Spread about 3 tablespoons of the sauce in the bottom of the dish. Layer 4 lasagna noodles, slightly overlapping, in the dish. Spread with one-third of the filling and sprinkle with one-third of the mozzarella. Repeat with two more layers of the noodles, filling, and mozzarella. Top with a final layer of noodles (you will have some left over). Spread with the remaining sauce, sprinkle with the Parmesan, and dot with the butter. (The lasagna can be prepared up to 1 day ahead, cooled, covered, and refrigerated.)

7. Position a rack in the center of the oven and preheat to 350°F. Place the baking dish on a rimmed baking sheet. Bake until the sauce is bubbling and tinged with golden brown, 40 to 45 minutes. Let stand for 10 minutes, then serve hot.

Note

To toast walnuts, spread the nuts on a rimmed baking sheet. Bake in a preheated 350°F oven, stirring occasionally, until toasted and fragrant, about 10 minutes. Cool completely before chopping.

Cheese Ravioli with Wild Mushroom and Marsala Sauce

Makes 4 to 6 servings

My neighbor Josephine de Pietro runs the best Italian delicatessen in our area, and they make their own ravioli. I find it hard to pass up a bowl of plump, cheese-filled ravioli under any circumstances, but when they are handmade, there's no turning back. Instead of the familiar tomato sauce, serve this robust mushroom topping, which is perfect for the winter season.

WILD MUSHROOM AND MARSALA SAUCE

2 tablespoons pure olive oil, plus more as needed

10 ounces cremini mushrooms, thickly sliced

10 ounces shiitake mushrooms, stems removed, caps thickly sliced

2 tablespoons unsalted butter

1 medium onion, finely chopped

2 garlic cloves, finely chopped

2 tablespoons tomato paste

½ cup dry Marsala (see Note)

1¼ cups beef or chicken stock, preferably homemade, or use canned low-sodium broth

¼ cup heavy cream

1 teaspoon chopped fresh rosemary, plus more for garnish

1¼ teaspoons cornstarch

Salt and freshly ground black pepper

Two 13-ounce packages large cheese ravioli (24 ravioli)

Freshly grated Parmesan, for serving

1. To make the mushroom sauce, heat the oil in a large skillet over medium-high heat. In batches, add the mushrooms and cook, stirring occasionally, adding more oil as needed, until they give off their juices and begin to brown, about 5 minutes. Transfer to a bowl.

2. Add the butter to the skillet and heat. Add the onion and cook, stirring often, until softened, about 3 minutes. Stir in the garlic and cook until it gives off its fragrance, about 1 minute. Dissolve the tomato paste in the Marsala and stir into the skillet. Increase the heat to high and boil the wine until it is reduced by half, about 1 minute.

3. Combine the stock, cream, and rosemary in a small bowl. Sprinkle in the cornstarch and stir to dissolve. Return the mushrooms to the skillet and pour in the stock mixture. Bring to a boil and reduce the heat to low. Simmer for 5 minutes to blend the flavors. Season with salt and pepper to taste. (The sauce can be made to this point up to 2 hours ahead. Reheat before continuing.)

4. Meanwhile, bring a large pot of salted water to a boil. Add the ravioli and cook, stirring occasionally, according to the package directions, until tender. Drain well. Return to the pot, add the sauce, and stir gently.

5. Spoon the ravioli into soup bowls and garnish with a sprinkle of rosemary. Serve hot, with the Parmesan on the side.

Note

Marsala, originally a fortified wine from Sicily, is similar to sherry. Bakers use sweet Marsala to make tiramisù and other Italian-style desserts. For savory dishes, such as this one, or the ubiquitous Chicken Marsala you find on many Italian-American menus, it is better to use dry Marsala, which has a less cloying flavor. Madeira or a dry sherry is a good substitute.

Homemade Spaetzle with Herb Butter

Makes 4 to 6 servings

When pressed for a side dish, I often throw together a batch of spaetzle, which could be considered the German answer to homemade pasta. The little noodle blobs are perfect for soaking up gravy, and I always try to serve them with sauerbraten. If you don't already own one, get an inexpensive spaetzle maker online or at a well-stocked kitchenware shop. Some recipes say you can drip the batter through a colander into boiling water to shape the spaetzle, but that is wishful thinking.

2 cups all-purpose flour

1 teaspoon salt

¼ teaspoon freshly ground black pepper

1½ cups whole milk

2 large eggs

2 tablespoons unsalted butter

2 tablespoons finely chopped fresh parsley or chives, or a combination

1. Bring a large saucepan of salted water to a boil over high heat.

2. Whisk the flour, salt, and pepper in a medium bowl and make a well in the center. In another bowl, whisk the milk and eggs together until combined. Pour into the well and whisk until smooth and the consistency of pancake batter.

3. Place the spaetzle maker over the boiling water. Pour the batter into the hopper and move it back and forth to force the batter through the holes into the water. When all of the batter has been added, let cook until the spaetzle rise to the surface, and then cook for 1 minute. Drain well. (The spaetzle can be prepared up to 2 hours ahead. Rinse them well with cold running water, then toss with 1 tablespoon vegetable oil to keep them from sticking together.)

4. Heat the butter in a large nonstick skillet over medium-high heat until the foam subsides. Add the spaetzle and cook, stirring occasionally, until heated through, about 2 minutes (or 5 minutes for room-temperature spaetzle). Sprinkle with the parsley and season with salt and pepper. Serve hot.

SIDE DISHES

Latkes with Apple-Jalapeño Salsa

Mashed Roots with Crispy Shallots

Potato and Garlic Gratin

Root Vegetables Anna

Mashed Potato Casserole with Smoked Gouda and Bacon

Mom's Red Cabbage

Five-Spice Applesauce

Braised Kale with Cornmeal Dumplings

Latkes with Apple-Jalapeño Salsa

Makes 12 latkes

Hanukkah is almost always celebrated in late fall, but it is considered a winter holiday. Even though I am not Jewish, I still look forward to my annual reason to dig into a plate of latkes, the potato pancakes that are the classic Hanukkah dish. I serve both this jazzed-up apple condiment as well as the more old-fashioned Five-Spice Applesauce on page 135. One important tip: Don't skimp on the oil, as latkes are supposed to be *fried*.

APPLE-JALAPEÑO SALSA

1 Granny Smith apple, peeled, cored, and finely diced

2 teaspoons fresh lime juice

1 tablespoon finely chopped shallots

1 jalapeño, seeds and ribs removed, finely chopped

1 tablespoon honey

1 tablespoon finely chopped fresh cilantro

Pinch of salt

LATKES

2 pounds baking potatoes, peeled

1 medium onion

2 large eggs, beaten

2 tablespoons matzo meal or dried bread crumbs

1 teaspoon salt

¼ teaspoon freshly ground black pepper

Vegetable oil, for frying

Sour cream, for serving

1. To make the salsa, combine the apple and lime juice in a small bowl. Add the shallots, jalapeño, honey, cilantro, and salt, and mix. Set aside at room temperature while making the latkes.

2. To make the latkes, position a rack in the center of the oven and preheat to 200°F. Line a baking sheet with a wire cake rack.

3. Shred the potatoes on the large holes of a box grater into a bowl. Grate the onions into the bowl. (Or, use a food processor to grate the potatoes and onions.) Add the eggs, matzo meal, salt, and pepper, and mix well. Do not be concerned if the potatoes discolor.

4. Pour enough oil into a large skillet to come about $\frac{1}{8}$ inch up the side and heat over medium-high heat until the oil shimmers. Using about $\frac{1}{4}$ cup of the potato mixture for each pancake, spoon into the oil and spread into 3-inch-diameter pancakes. Cook until the underside is golden brown, about $2\frac{1}{2}$ minutes. Turn and cook until the other side is brown, about $2\frac{1}{2}$ minutes more. Transfer to the rack and keep warm in the oven while making the remaining latkes.

5. Just before serving, transfer the latkes to paper towels to drain. (If the latkes remain on the paper towels more than a minute or so, they will get soggy.) Serve immediately, with the salsa and sour cream on the side.

Mashed Roots with Crispy Shallots

Makes 6 servings

Mashed potatoes have their place, but often this earthy mix of carrots, parsnips, and potatoes is even more satisfying. It is certainly more colorful! Topped with a tangle of golden brown shallots, it will have everyone asking for seconds.

MASHED ROOTS

1 pound carrots, peeled and cut into ½-inch-thick rounds

1 pound parsnips, peeled and cut into ½-inch-thick rounds

1 pound baking potatoes, such as russet or Burbank, peeled and cut into 1-inch chunks

3 tablespoons unsalted butter

3 tablespoons heavy cream, as needed

Salt and freshly ground black pepper

CRISPY SHALLOTS

Vegetable oil, for frying

2 shallots, cut crosswise into thin rounds, separated into rings

¼ cup all-purpose flour

1. To prepare the mashed roots, combine the carrots, parsnips, and potatoes in a large saucepan, and add enough salted water to cover. Bring to a boil over high heat. Reduce the heat to medium-low and simmer until tender, about 25 minutes.

2. Drain well and return the vegetables to the saucepan. Cook over medium-low heat, stirring constantly, until they begin to film the bottom of the pan, about 2 minutes.

3. Remove from the heat. Add the butter and mash, adding enough heavy cream to reach the desired consistency. Season with salt and pepper to taste. Cover tightly to keep warm.

4. To make the shallots, line a baking sheet with paper towels. Pour enough oil into a large saucepan to come 1 inch up the side. Heat over high heat until the oil is shimmering. Toss the shallots with the flour and shake off the excess flour. Add the shallots to the oil and cook until golden brown, about 15 seconds. (Do a test run first with a few shallot rings to check the oil temperature.) Using a wire skimmer, lift the shallots out of the oil and drain briefly on paper towels.

5. Transfer the mashed roots to a serving dish, top with the crispy shallots, and serve immediately.

Potato and Garlic Gratin

Makes 8 servings

Every year at Christmas dinner, I have to serve this gratin by popular demand. Even though I have recipes for gratins with much bolder flavor profiles, there must be something about the simplicity of the combination of potatoes, cream, and garlic that makes this one so comforting. Yes, it takes an entire quart of cream, but that is the secret to the recipe. If someone asks why this is so much better than their scalloped potatoes, do what I do—fib about the amount of cream. The gratin takes some time to cook, so don't rush it.

1 quart heavy cream

6 garlic cloves, coarsely chopped

2½ teaspoons salt

½ teaspoon freshly ground black pepper

3 pounds baking potatoes, such as russet or Burbank, peeled and cut into ⅛-inch-thick rounds (see Note)

1. Position a rack in the center of the oven and preheat to 375°F. Lightly butter a 13 x 9-inch baking dish.

2. Slowly bring the cream and garlic to a simmer in a medium saucepan over medium-low heat, taking care that the cream doesn't boil over. Remove from the heat.

3. Mix the salt and pepper together. Layer half of the potato rounds, overlapping as needed, in the baking dish. Using a slotted spoon, remove the garlic from the cream and scatter the garlic over the potatoes. Season with half of the salt and pepper

mixture. Layer the remaining potatoes in the dish and season with the remaining salt and pepper mixture. Pour the hot cream evenly over the potatoes. Cover the dish with aluminum foil.

4. Place the baking dish on a rimmed baking sheet. Bake for 45 minutes. Remove the foil. Bake until the potatoes are tender when pierced with the tip of a sharp knife and the top of the gratin is golden brown, about 45 minutes longer. Let stand for 5 minutes, then serve hot.

Note

An inexpensive V-shaped slicer (which I find so much easier to use than the classic metal mandoline) will cut the potatoes into uniformly thin rounds, and is a good addition to your kitchen if you don't already own one. Or buy narrow potatoes that will fit into the feed tube of a food processor, and cut them with the slicing blade. Of course the potatoes can be sliced by hand with a large knife, but be sure to cut them thinly, or they will take forever to cook to tenderness.

Root Vegetables Anna

Makes 6 servings

This is an elegant presentation for humble root vegetables—a crisp outer shell of thinly sliced potatoes enclosing a tender filling of sweet celery root and earthy turnips. A mandoline or food processor will make short work of the slicing.

3 baking potatoes, such as russet or Burbank (1¼ pounds)

½ medium celery root (also known as celeriac)

1 medium turnip

6 tablespoons unsalted butter

1 teaspoon salt

½ teaspoon freshly ground black pepper

1 teaspoon chopped fresh rosemary

1. Preheat the oven to 400°F.

2. Peel the potatoes, celery root, and turnip. Using a V-shaped slicer or food processor, cut the potatoes into ⅛-inch-thick rounds. Place in a bowl, but do not rinse or cover with water. Repeat with the celery root and turnip; you should have about 2 cups combined celery root and turnip.

3. Immediately melt the butter in a 9-inch-diameter nonstick skillet over medium heat. Pour out all but 2 tablespoons of the butter into a heatproof bowl. Arrange half of the potatoes in concentric circles in the skillet. Season with half of the salt and pepper. Arrange the celery root and turnip over the potatoes and sprinkle with the rosemary.

Drizzle with 2 tablespoons of the remaining butter and half of the remaining salt and pepper. Top with the remaining potatoes and salt and pepper. Press the vegetables with your hands to make an even thickness. Reduce the heat to medium-low and cover tightly, preferably with a flat, and not domed, lid. Cook until the bottom layer of the potatoes is golden brown, about 20 minutes.

4. Holding the lid and skillet together, invert to unmold the root vegetable "cake" onto the lid. (If your skillet lid is domed, substitute a large, flat plate when inverting the vegetables.) Pour the remaining butter into the skillet and swirl the skillet to coat the inside with butter. Slide the cake off the lid and back into the skillet, browned side up. If the skillet handle is not heatproof, wrap in aluminum foil.

5. Place the cake in the oven and bake until the vegetables are tender when pierced with a sharp knife, about 30 minutes. Slide onto a platter, cut into wedges, and serve.

Root Vegetables

Nature works in very mysterious ways. Just when the delicate fruits and vegetables of summer are depleted, another source of food appears to give us sustenance. These are the root vegetables, which feed humans throughout the cold, barren winter until spring's bounty emerges.

Not all of a plant is edible. Sometimes we eat only the leaves, or just the fruit that contains the seeds that regenerate the plant. With others, the root that grows under the ground is the edible part. Roots collect the moisture in the ground and send it up to the leaves. To retain this moisture, their skins are tough. Even though you may hear that you should not peel root vegetables in order to benefit from the vitamins in the skins, for the best texture, peel them.

When the roots are pulled up, these same tough skins are actually beneficial, because they allow the vegetables to be kept for quite a while before drying out, even without the benefit of electrical refrigeration. The classic root cellar of the American farm was a cool, dark place where the vegetables could be stored throughout the long, cold winter. Some vegetables are commonly considered root vegetables even though they are tubers (potatoes and beets, for example), where the edible portions grow between the leaves and the roots.

Root vegetables are sweet because they also are the receptacle for the plants' starches, which are converted into sugars by enzymes. Many recipes for root vegetables play up this inherent sweetness with a little added sugar. Roasting is one of the best ways to cook root vegetables because browning brings out the sugary flavors.

Mashed Potato Casserole with Smoked Gouda and Bacon

Makes 6 to 8 servings

This casserole was created as an over-the-top potato accompaniment for a simply prepared pork loin or roast chicken. It has a double dose of smoked ingredients with both bacon and smoked Gouda. A crunchy bacon-and-scallion topping acts as a counterpoint to the creamy potatoes, and is part of this dish's charm.

> 6 bacon strips, preferably thick-sliced applewood smoked
>
> 3 scallions, green and white parts, finely chopped
>
> 3 pounds baking potatoes, such as russet or Burbank, peeled and cut into 2-inch chunks
>
> 4 tablespoons (½ stick) unsalted butter, plus more for the baking dish
>
> ¾ cup sour cream
>
> ⅓ cup milk
>
> 2 cups (8 ounces) shredded smoked Gouda

1. Cook the bacon in a large skillet over medium heat, turning occasionally, until crisp and brown, about 10 minutes. Transfer to paper towels to drain and cool. Chop the cooked bacon. Combine the bacon and scallions; set aside.

2. Place the potatoes in a large saucepan and add enough cold salted water to cover. Cover the saucepan with a lid and bring to a boil over high heat. Reduce the heat to medium and cook with the lid ajar until the potatoes are tender, 20 to 25 minutes. Drain well. Return the potatoes to the empty saucepan. Cook over low heat, stirring often, until the potatoes film the bottom of the saucepan, about 2 minutes.

3. Butter a 13 x 9-inch baking dish. Add the butter, sour cream, and milk to the potatoes. Mash with a potato masher (or beat with an electric hand mixer on low speed) until smooth. Stir in 1½ cups of the Gouda and two-thirds of the bacon mixture; reserve the remaining bacon mixture. Spread in the baking dish. Sprinkle the remaining ½ cup Gouda on top. (The casserole and the bacon mixture can be prepared up to 8 hours ahead, but keep them separately covered and refrigerated. Remove the bacon mixture from the refrigerator 1 hour before serving.)

4. Preheat the oven to 350°F. Bake until the cheese melts and the edges of the mashed potatoes are bubbling, about 30 minutes (or about 40 minutes if refrigerated). Sprinkle with the reserved bacon mixture and serve hot.

Mom's Red Cabbage

Makes 8 servings

This is based on my mom's red cabbage, which, in turn, comes from her mother's version. Of course, like most all mothers, Mom isn't too concerned about measurements or even precise ingredients. Sometimes she'll substitute fruit preserves or even Chinese plum sauce for some of the sugar. This makes a healthy amount of cabbage, but that's okay, because leftovers are even better than freshly made.

2 bacon strips, coarsely chopped

2 teaspoons vegetable oil

2 Granny Smith apples, peeled, cored, and cut into ½-inch dice

1 medium onion, chopped

One 2½-pound head red cabbage, cored and cut into thin shreds

½ cup red wine vinegar

½ cup packed light brown sugar

1 teaspoon dried thyme

1 bay leaf

Salt and freshly ground black pepper

1. Cook the bacon and oil together in a large saucepan over medium heat, stirring occasionally, until the bacon is crisp and browned, about 8 minutes. Using a slotted spoon, transfer the bacon to paper towels, leaving the fat in the saucepan.

2. Add the apples to the saucepan and cook, stirring occasionally, until they begin to brown, about 5 minutes. Stir in the onion and cook until softened, about 3 minutes.

Add the cabbage and vinegar, and stir well. Add the brown sugar, thyme, and bay leaf, and stir again. Return the bacon to the saucepan. Reduce the heat to medium-low and cover. Simmer, stirring occasionally, until the cabbage is very tender, about 1¼ hours.

3. Remove the bay leaf. Season with salt and pepper to taste and serve hot.

Five-Spice Applesauce

Makes about 5 cups

Making applesauce is a winter tradition for many cooks, and I like to have a container in the refrigerator for serving with pork chops, roast turkey, and, of course, latkes. You can make applesauce of just about any apple, or combination, as long as you avoid Red Delicious, which melt into a glop. And a little wine or hard cider and interesting Asian-style spicing elevates this applesauce from Grandma's.

1 whole star anise

¼ teaspoon Sichuan peppercorns

⅛ teaspoon fennel seed

¼ teaspoon ground cinnamon

⅛ teaspoon ground cloves

3 pounds all-purpose apples, such as Macoun, Cortland, or Golden Delicious, peeled, cored, and cut into 1-inch chunks

½ cup semidry white wine, such as Riesling, hard cider, or water

⅓ cup sugar

2 tablespoons fresh lemon juice

1. Grind the star anise, peppercorns, and fennel seed in an electric spice grinder or in a mortar. Add the cinnamon and cloves. Sift through a fine-mesh wire sieve to remove any hard bark.

2. Combine the apples, wine, sugar, spices, and lemon juice in a heavy-bottomed medium saucepan. Bring to a boil over medium heat. Cook, stirring often (the harder you stir, the more the apples will break down), until the apples have formed a thick, chunky sauce, about 15 minutes.

3. Serve warm or cooled to room temperature. (The applesauce can be cooled, covered, and refrigerated for up to 5 days.)

Braised Kale with Cornmeal Dumplings

Makes 6 to 8 servings

I devised this pot of greens with tender cornmeal dumplings as a side dish for Southern-inspired main courses like baked ham and fried chicken. It makes a lot, but I don't mind, because leftovers are quickly transformed into soup with some chicken or pork stock. My market carries three kinds of kale: bright green standard kale, dark green curly kale, and the very dark Italian "dinosaur" kale also known as *cavolo nero*. Use the one you like, or even a combination.

BRAISED KALE

2½ pounds kale

3 bacon strips, coarsely chopped

2 teaspoons vegetable oil

1 medium onion, chopped

1 medium celery rib, chopped

½ green bell pepper, seeds and ribs removed, chopped

2 garlic cloves, finely chopped

3 cups chicken stock, preferably homemade, or use canned low-sodium broth

2 tablespoons cider vinegar

1 teaspoon crushed hot red pepper flakes

Salt and freshly ground black pepper

Cornmeal Dumplings

1 cup all-purpose flour

½ cup yellow cornmeal, preferably stone-ground

2 teaspoons baking powder

1 teaspoon sugar

½ teaspoon salt

¾ cup whole milk

½ cup thawed frozen corn kernels

1. To prepare the kale, remove the tough stems. Chop the stems into ½-inch-thick pieces. Fill a sink with cold water and add the stems. Wash the stems well. Lift out of the water and set aside in a bowl; do not dry. Fill the sink with fresh water. A few at a time, stack the leaves and cut crosswise into ½-inch-wide strips. Add to the water and wash well. Lift out of the water and transfer to a large colander; do not dry.

2. Cook the bacon and oil in a large saucepan over medium heat, stirring occasionally, until the bacon is crisp and browned, about 8 minutes. Using a slotted spoon, transfer the bacon to paper towels to drain, leaving the fat in the saucepan.

3. Add the onion, celery, and green pepper to the saucepan and cook, stirring occasionally, until softened, about 3 minutes. Stir in the garlic and cook until it gives off its fragrance, about 1 minute. Stir in the stems. In batches, add the leaves, letting the first batch wilt before adding another. Stir in the stock, vinegar, and red pepper flakes, and bring to a boil. Reduce the heat to medium-low and simmer until the leaves are tender, about 30 minutes. Season with salt and pepper to taste.

4. To make the dumplings, whisk the flour, cornmeal, baking powder, sugar, and salt together in a medium bowl. Add the milk and stir until combined. Stir in the corn. Drop the batter by heaping teaspoons into the saucepan—you should have 24 small dumplings. Cover and simmer until the dumplings are cooked through, about 15 minutes.

5. To serve, spoon the kale with its liquid and the dumplings into individual bowls and serve hot. (You can also serve the kale and dumplings with a slotted spoon, and pour the cooking liquid into mugs to sip on the side.)

DESSERTS ❄

Homemade Marshmallows

Butterscotch Banana Pudding

Kumquat Upside-Down Cake

Chocolate and Orange Tart

Pear Soufflés "Hélène"

Maple Crèmes Brûlées

Grapefruit Cupcakes

Pear and Crystallized Ginger Gingerbread

Homemade Marshmallows

Makes about 1 pound, 24 large marshmallows

What could be cooler to make at home than marshmallows? They are really very easy to pull off, as long as you have the right tools—a candy thermometer and a heavy-duty standing mixer. Make a batch to put on top of a steaming mug of hot chocolate (page 20), or give them away as holiday gifts.

Vegetable oil for the pan

Confectioners' sugar for the pan and the work surface

2 envelopes (4 teaspoons) unflavored gelatin

1 cup granulated sugar

⅔ cup light corn syrup

⅛ teaspoon salt

2 teaspoons vanilla extract

1. Lightly oil an 8-inch square baking pan. Line the bottom and the two short sides with a strip of aluminum foil, preferably nonstick, folding the excess foil over the edges to act as handles. Lightly oil the foil. Generously dust the bottom and the sides of the pan with confectioners' sugar.

2. Pour ⅓ cup water in the bowl of a heavy-duty electric mixer and sprinkle the gelatin on top. Attach the bowl to the mixer and affix the paddle blade.

3. Combine the granulated sugar, corn syrup, and an additional ⅓ cup water in a small saucepan. Attach a candy thermometer to the pan. Bring to a boil over high heat, stirring to dissolve the sugar. When the syrup boils, stop stirring and boil, washing

down any sugar crystals that form on the sides of the pan with a pastry brush dipped in cold water and occasionally swirling the pan by the handle, until the syrup reaches 240°F.

4. With the mixer on low speed, gradually pour the hot syrup into the gelatin mixture. After the syrup has been added, add the salt and increase the speed to medium-high. Beat until the mixture is white, fluffy, and cooled to tepid, 8 to 10 minutes. Beat in the vanilla.

5. Rinse a rubber spatula under cold water. Using the wet spatula, immediately spread the mixture in the prepared pan. Let stand until completely set, at least 4 hours. Generously dust a work surface with confectioners' sugar. Invert and unmold the marshmallow onto the work surface and peel off the foil. Using an oiled knife or pizza wheel, cut into 24 pieces. (The marshmallows can be stored in an airtight container for up to 1 week.)

Butterscotch Banana Pudding

Because they are always reliably tasty, bananas are a good fruit to use in winter desserts. I love banana pudding as much as the next guy, if not more. Over the years, I've fooled around with the recipe to get away from the plain vanilla version. This is my latest rendition, with the caramel flavor of butterscotch and the spiciness of gingersnaps to perk up the bananas.

BUTTERSCOTCH PUDDING

6 tablespoons (¾ stick) unsalted butter, divided

¾ cup packed light or dark brown sugar (use dark for a deeper molasses flavor)

1 cup heavy cream

¼ cup cornstarch

2 cups whole milk

4 large egg yolks

1 teaspoon vanilla extract

2 ripe bananas, peeled and sliced

1½ cups coarsely crushed gingersnap cookies

½ cup heavy cream

1 tablespoon granulated sugar

½ teaspoon vanilla extract

1. To make the pudding, melt 4 tablespoons of the butter in a heavy-bottomed medium saucepan over medium heat. Add the brown sugar and whisk until the mixture is melted. Whisk in the heavy cream and cook until the mixture comes to a simmer.

2. Sprinkle the cornstarch over the milk and whisk until dissolved. Whisk into the saucepan and cook until it comes to a simmer. Whisk the egg yolks together in a heatproof medium bowl. Gradually whisk in about 1 cup of the hot cream mixture, then whisk it back into the saucepan. Cook, whisking constantly, until the pudding comes to a full boil. Reduce the heat to low and whisk for another 15 seconds. (Be sure that the pudding comes to a full lavalike boil, or it will thin out as it stands.) Remove from the heat. Whisk in the vanilla. Transfer to a bowl. Cut the remaining 2 tablespoons butter into small cubes and scatter over the top of the pudding. Cover the pudding with a sheet of plastic wrap pressed directly on the surface. Pierce a few slits in the plastic wrap with the tip of a small knife and let cool.

3. Layer the pudding, bananas, and gingersnaps in 6 dessert bowls or glasses. Cover each with a piece of plastic wrap pressed directly on the surface of the pudding and refrigerate until chilled, at least 2 hours.

4. Whip the cream, granulated sugar, and vanilla in a chilled medium bowl with a hand-held electric mixer on high speed until stiff peaks form. Top each pudding with a dollop of the cream and serve chilled.

Kumquat Upside-Down Cake

Upside-down cakes are unabashedly old-fashioned, but they sure make an impressive dessert. As kumquats are an underappreciated fruit that no one seems to know what to do with, this cake has another built-in chance to impress your guests with an unfamiliar ingredient. And with its glistening rounds of orange kumquats, it looks fantastic, too. As it takes guts to unmold the cake out of a heavy cast-iron skillet, substitute a heavy-gauge 10 x 2-inch metal cake pan, if you prefer.

KUMQUAT TOPPING

1 pint kumquats

1 cup packed light brown sugar

6 tablespoons (¾ stick) unsalted butter, cut into small pieces

CAKE

1½ cups all-purpose flour

1 cup granulated sugar

1½ teaspoons baking powder

¼ teaspoon salt

8 tablespoons (1 stick) unsalted butter, at very soft room temperature

½ cup milk

2 large eggs, at room temperature

1 teaspoon vanilla extract

1. Position a rack in the center of the oven and preheat to 350°F.

2. To make the kumquat topping, cut each kumquat crosswise into thirds, removing the seeds. Stir the brown sugar and butter in a 9- to 10-inch-diameter cast-iron skillet over medium heat until the sugar is melted and bubbling. Add the kumquats and spread them out in the sugar mixture in a single layer.

3. To make the cake, whisk the flour, granulated sugar, baking powder, and salt in a medium bowl. Add the butter, milk, eggs, and vanilla. Mix with an electric mixer set on low speed to moisten. Increase the speed to high and mix, scraping down the sides of the bowl with a rubber spatula as needed, for 2 minutes (set a timer to be sure), until smooth and fluffy. Scrape into the skillet and smooth the top.

4. Bake until the cake is golden brown and springs back when pressed lightly in the center with your finger, about 35 minutes. Let stand in the pan on a wire cake rack for 5 minutes.

5. Run a knife around the inside of the skillet to release the cake. Place a round rimmed serving platter over the pan. Holding the platter and skillet together, quickly invert to unmold the cake. Let stand until warm or cool completely. Cut into wedges and serve.

Kumquats

Looking like small, elongated oranges, attached to glossy dark green leaves, kumquats are so attractive that when I first came across them at the market, I used them mainly for garnishing. It was my loss that it took me a while to discover how delicious they can be in cooking.

Kumquats are originally from China, and didn't really make it to the West until the mid-nineteenth century, and even then, they were appreciated more for their beauty in the garden than in the kitchen. There is quite an argument between botanists whether kumquats belong to their own genus, *Fortunella,* or if they are a member of the *Citrus* family. They are frost-hardy, and thrive in cool areas like the San Francisco Bay Area.

The entire fruit is edible, although eating is easier if the seeds are removed. While one could simply serve sliced kumquats macerated in sugar or liqueur, I prefer to cook them to soften their texture and mellow their tartness. Try adding them to home-made cranberry sauce, or simmering them on their own with some sugar to make a quick warm topping for ice cream.

Chocolate and Orange Tart

Makes 8 servings

Every baker needs a surefire showstopper, something guaranteed to garner
oohs and aahs from dinner guests, and this tart is one of my tried-and-trues.
First of all, it's hard to find someone who doesn't love chocolate. Second, it
is very easy to make—the pastry crust doesn't even require rolling out. The
color combination of deep brown chocolate and neon-bright orange segments
is dramatic, especially when you use both navel and blood oranges. Consider
making this for Valentine's Day.

CRUST

1 cup all-purpose flour

3 tablespoons sugar

¼ teaspoon salt

6 tablespoons (¾ stick) unsalted butter, thinly sliced

1 large egg yolk, beaten with 1 tablespoon water

FILLING

5 oranges, preferably a combination of navel and blood oranges

1½ cups heavy cream

9 ounces bittersweet chocolate, finely chopped

3 tablespoons unsalted butter, at room temperature

1 tablespoon light corn syrup

1. To make the crust, pulse the flour, sugar, and salt together in a food processor fitted
   with the metal chopping blade to combine. Add the butter and pulse about 8 times
   until the mixture resembles coarse crumbs. With the machine running, add the yolk

mixture and pulse just until the mixture clumps together. Transfer to a 9-inch tart pan with a removable bottom. Firmly and evenly press the dough into the bottom and up the sides of the pan. Pierce the dough all over with a fork. Freeze for 30 minutes.

2. Position a rack in the center of the oven and preheat to 400°F. Place the tart pan on a rimmed baking sheet. Line the dough with aluminum foil and fill with pie weights or dried beans. Bake until the exposed edge of the crust looks set and is beginning to brown, about 15 minutes. Lift off the foil with the weights. Continue baking until the crust is golden brown, about 15 minutes more. Transfer to a wire cake rack and let cool completely.

3. To make the filling, grate the zest from 1 orange and set aside. Cut off the peel from each orange. Working over a bowl to catch the segments and juice, using a serrated knife, cut between the membranes to release the segments. Cover and refrigerate the oranges and juice until ready to serve.

4. Bring the cream to a simmer in a heavy medium saucepan. Remove from the heat and add the chocolate. Let stand until the chocolate softens, about 3 minutes. Whisk until smooth. Add the butter, corn syrup, and orange zest, and whisk again. Pour into the cooled crust and smooth the top. Refrigerate until the filling is set, at least 1 hour. (The tart can be refrigerated, uncovered, for up to 1 day.)

5. Just before serving, drain the orange segments (drink the juice as the chef's treat), and pat them dry on paper towels. Arrange the orange segments on the chocolate filling. Cut into wedges and serve chilled.

Blood Oranges

One morning in Italy, my breakfast glass of orange juice was a shocking deep red color, and the flavor was less acidic than usual, with hints of berries. I had just been introduced to blood oranges.

At that time, there were only two kinds of American oranges—the California navel orange (the first choice for eating) and the Florida Valencia juice orange. I learned that the Italian oranges were actually Tarocco oranges from Sicily. If I had had my first blood orange experience in Spain, I surely would have been served the Spanish variety, called Sanguinello (*sangue* is Spanish for blood). The oranges get their dramatic red hue from anthocyanin, a pigment that is found in red flowers and plants, but isn't common in fruits.

A few years ago, I noticed that the blood orange, like so many other Italian foods, had made the jump over the Atlantic. Farmers in California were growing a new strain of blood orange, the Moro. Later, a second blood orange found its way into the market, the Cara Cara. Most people won't care about the difference, but the Cara Cara isn't a true blood orange, it is a mutation and its color comes from lycopene, the same pigment/antitoxicant that colors papaya, tomatoes, and watermelon.

The season for blood oranges runs from November to May, with its peak in January and February. They are great fun to cook with, for with their unexpected color and berrylike flavor, they always end up being a subject of conversation.

Pear Soufflés "Hélène"

My friend and *Bon Appétit* food editor Kristine Kidd is very selective about her dessert calories, so when she reported that she ate her entire helping of this elegant soufflé, I knew I had a winner. It is a reconstructed version of the classic bistro dessert Poires Hélène, poached pears with chocolate sauce. For the best results, the pears must be very ripe and juicy, so buy them a few days ahead and let ripen at room temperature.

CHOCOLATE-COGNAC SAUCE

⅔ cup heavy cream

5 ounces bittersweet chocolate, finely chopped

2 tablespoons Cognac, brandy, or pear liqueur

SOUFFLÉS

2 tablespoons unsalted butter, plus more for the soufflé dishes

5 ripe Comice or Anjou pears (about 2½ pounds total), peeled, cored, and cut into ½-inch dice

½ cup sugar, divided, plus more for the soufflé dishes

2 teaspoons fresh lemon juice

3 large eggs, separated, plus 1 large egg white, at room temperature

1. To make the sauce, heat the cream in a medium saucepan over medium-low heat until simmering. Remove from the heat. Add the chocolate and let stand until chocolate softens, about 3 minutes. Add the Cognac and whisk until smooth. (The sauce can be made 1 day ahead, covered, and stored at room temperature.) Set the sauce aside.

2. To make the soufflés, butter the insides of six ³/₄-cup soufflé dishes or ramekins. Coat the insides with sugar and tap out the excess. Place on a rimmed baking sheet.

3. Melt 1 tablespoon of the butter in a large nonstick skillet over medium-high heat. Add half of the pears and cook, stirring occasionally, until they begin to brown around the edges, about 6 minutes. Sprinkle with 1½ tablespoons sugar and cook until the pears are caramelized and the juices are thick, about 3 minutes longer. Transfer to a bowl. Repeat with the remaining butter, pears, and another 1½ tablespoons of the sugar. Stir in the lemon juice.

4. Using a slotted spoon, transfer all of the pears to a food processor or blender, reserving the pear juice in the bowl. Puree the pears. (The puree can be prepared up to 2 days ahead, covered and refrigerated.)

5. Transfer the puree to a heavy-bottomed medium saucepan. Whisk the egg yolks into the puree. Heat over medium-low heat, stirring constantly, until the mixture is very hot but not boiling. Transfer to a medium bowl.

6. Beat the egg whites in a separate medium bowl with a hand-held electric mixer set on high speed just until soft peaks form. One tablespoon at a time, beat in the remaining 5 tablespoons sugar and beat just until shiny peaks form. Stir one-fourth of the whites into the pear mixture to lighten it, then fold in the remaining whites. Spoon into the prepared dishes (the dishes will be full).

7. Position a rack in the center of the oven and preheat to 375°F. Bake until the soufflés are puffed and golden brown, about 15 minutes. Meanwhile, stir 2 tablespoons of the reserved pear juice into the chocolate sauce and gently reheat the sauce over low heat just until warm; do not boil. Pour into a sauceboat. Serve the soufflés immediately, with the chocolate sauce served on the side. Allow each guest to pierce a hole in the center of their soufflé and pour in the sauce.

Pears

In order to develop their full flavor, pears need cool evenings, which extends their growing season well into the fall, and they store deep into the winter. Most American pears are grown in Oregon, Washington, and northern California, and are shipped throughout the country, although you will find some locally grown pears outside of these major growing regions.

Pears are one of the few fruits that are meant to be ripened off the tree, as they turn gritty otherwise. So plan ahead when serving pears, as you will rarely find ripe ones at the market. Bring them home and let them ripen at room temperature until they have a slight give when pressed at the neck, a process that takes a few days. To hasten ripening, close them in a paper bag with bananas to trap the ethylene gas the fruits give off. Never refrigerate pears until they have reached the desired state of ripeness.

Pears are often nicked during shipping from the stems on the other fruits in the box (for this reason, expensive "fancy" pears are hand-wrapped in tissue and

nestled individually in boxes before transporting), so if you want perfect pears for presentation, choose them carefully.

You will find quite a range of flavors and textures in the pear varieties, which arrive at different points of the season. Bartletts (with either yellow or red skins) and Anjous (green or red) are juicy and sweet and wonderful for eating out of hand. Comice pears are larger and loaded with honeylike juice. Firm, russet-colored Boscs are good for baking because they hold their shape after heating. Small Seckle or Forelles are great for serving on cheese platters, as their small size makes for nice individual servings.

Maple Crèmes Brûlées

Spoonful for spoonful, there are few culinary experiences more sensual than the silken feel of crème brûlée. Maple syrup, which can only be collected during fluctuations in cold winter weather, is a flavor that is associated with the cooler months. It adds its distinctive taste to these luxurious custards. Use Grade B syrup, which is more deeply flavored than Grade A. And while you can broil the custards to give them their caramelized sugar tops, an inexpensive kitchen torch (or even a propane torch from the hardware shop) is so efficient that you will want to make these often.

2½ cups heavy cream

6 large egg yolks

⅔ cup pure maple syrup, preferably Grade B

3 tablespoons bourbon or dark rum

6 teaspoons turbinado sugar

1. Position a rack in the center of the oven and preheat to 325°F.

2. Bring the cream to a simmer in a medium saucepan over medium heat. Whisk the egg yolks and syrup together in a large heatproof bowl. Gradually whisk in the hot cream and then the bourbon. Pour equal amounts into six ³⁄₄-cup ramekins. Place the ramekins in a roasting pan.

3. Place the roasting pan in the oven and pour in enough hot water to come a ½ inch up the sides of the ramekins. Bake until the custards are barely set (if you remove a ramekin from the oven and give it a gentle shake, the center will jiggle), about 40 minutes. Remove the ramekins from the water and let cool.

4. Wrap each custard in plastic wrap and refrigerate until chilled, at least 2 hours. (The custards can be made up to 1 day ahead.)

5. Sprinkle each custard with 1 teaspoon turbinado sugar. Holding the flame about 1 inch above the sugar, wave a kitchen torch back and forth over the sugar to melt it. Serve immediately to savor the contrasting hot and cold temperatures of the topping and the custard.

Maple Syrup

True maple syrup (as opposed to the artificially flavored glop that has done its best to replace the real thing) is an authentic winter ingredient. The sap from a maple tree can only be collected when the nighttime temperatures dip below freezing, and the daytime temperatures climb above that point. So, there will be snow on the ground when that happens—usually February through April. The temperature fluctuations disturb the moisture content in the tree, and make the sap flow. The collected sap is boiled and cooked down into syrup. To give you an idea of how time-consuming this hands-on process is, it takes about 40 quarts of sap to be boiled down to about 1 quart of syrup. When I learned this, I stopped complaining about maple syrup's high prices.

American syrup is divided into two categories: Grade A and Grade B. Within Grade A, which has a gentler maple flavor, are three colors: Light, Medium, and

Dark Amber. Grade B has a more pronounced maple flavor and is darker than Dark Amber.

The state of Vermont, which supplies the bulk of maple syrup in this country, has a slightly different grading system and adds the word "Fancy" to some designations. Vermont maple syrup's main distinction is that it is boiled to a slightly heavier viscosity than the syrup from other states and Canada.

Some cooks reserve Grade A for serving with breakfast foods like waffles and pancakes, and use Grade B for baking and cooking. Personally, because I like bold flavors, I prefer Grade B for whenever I use maple syrup. And it is relatively cheaper than Grade A, too.

Grapefruit Cupcakes

Another dessert that celebrates citrus fruit, the original version of this cake made its debut at Hollywood's famous Brown Derby decades ago. It deserves its celebrity—the sweet-and-sour combination of the cake and frosting with the grapefruit is wonderful. Lately, I've been making cupcakes more often than layer cakes, as the former are easier to decorate and lots of fun to eat out of hand, so I adapted my old recipe into these "cake-ettes."

CUPCAKES

1 large pink or red grapefruit

1⅓ cups cake flour

1¼ teaspoons baking powder

¼ teaspoon salt

¾ cup plus 2 tablespoons (1¾ sticks) unsalted butter, at room temperature

1 cup granulated sugar

4 large eggs, at room temperature

1 teaspoon vanilla extract

¼ cup whole milk

1 tablespoon confectioners' sugar

CREAM CHEESE ICING

6 ounces cream cheese, at soft room temperature

2 cups confectioners' sugar, sifted

2 teaspoons fresh grapefruit juice, as needed

Pink or red food coloring (optional)

1. To make the cupcakes, position a rack in the center of the over and preheat to 350°F. Line a 12-cup muffin pan with paper cupcake liners.

2. Grate the zest from half of the grapefruit and set aside. Cut off the peel and segment the grapefruit, working over a bowl to collect the juice. Set the 12 nicest segments (eat the rest of the segments as the cook's treat) and the juice aside.

3. Sift together the flour, baking powder, and salt. Using an electric mixer set on high speed, beat the butter and granulated sugar in a medium bowl until light in color and texture, about 3 minutes. One at a time, beat in the eggs, beating well after each addition, then beat in the reserved grapefruit zest and the vanilla. With the mixer on low speed, in three additions, alternating with two additions of milk, mix in the flour, scraping down the sides of the bowl as needed. Divide evenly among the muffin cups.

4. Bake until the cupcakes are golden brown and a toothpick inserted in the center comes out clean, about 20 minutes. Cool for 5 minutes. Remove the cupcakes from the pan and transfer to a wire cake rack and cool completely.

5. Whisk together ¼ cup of the reserved grapefruit juice and the confectioners' sugar. Brush the cupcakes with the grapefruit juice mixture.

6. To make the icing, using an electric mixer set on high speed, beat the cream cheese in a medium bowl until smooth. Reduce the heat to low and gradually add the confectioners' sugar. Add enough grapefruit juice to make a flowing but spreadable icing. Beat in food coloring to tint the icing pink, if desired. Spread each cupcake with the icing and top with a grapefruit section. (The cupcakes can be made up to 1 day ahead, covered loosely with plastic wrap and refrigerated. Remove from the refrigerator 1 hour before serving.)

Pear and Crystallized Ginger Gingerbread

For my money, gingerbread isn't worth baking unless it is good and spicy. Crystallized ginger is a good way to get intensely spicy flavor into baked goods. As pears are also compatible with warm spices, they are a natural addition to this comforting dessert. The gingerbread is as versatile as it is delicious, and can be eaten out of hand for a quick snack, or gussied up with warm caramel sauce and whipped cream for an impressive dessert.

3 ripe-firm Bartlett or Bosc pears, peeled, cored, and cut lengthwise into ½-inch-thick slices

2½ cups all-purpose flour

2 teaspoons baking soda

2 teaspoons ground ginger

1½ teaspoons ground cinnamon

½ teaspoon ground cloves

½ teaspoon salt

8 tablespoons (1 stick) unsalted butter, at room temperature, plus more for the baking pan

1 cup sugar

1 cup unsulfured (light) molasses

2 large eggs, at room temperature

1 cup boiling water

⅓ cup chopped crystallized ginger

1. Position a rack in the center of the oven and preheat to 350°F. Butter a 13 x 9-inch baking pan. Spread the pears in the pan.

2. Sift the flour, baking soda, ground ginger, cinnamon, cloves, and salt together. Beat the butter and sugar in a large bowl with a hand-held electric mixer set on high speed until the mixture is pale yellow, about 3 minutes. Beat in the molasses, then the eggs, one at a time.

3. With the mixer on low speed, beat in the flour mixture in three equal additions, alternating with two equal additions of the boiling water, scraping down the sides of the bowl with a rubber spatula as needed. The batter will be thin. Stir in the crystallized ginger. Pour into the pan.

4. Bake until a toothpick inserted in the center of the gingerbread comes out clean, about 35 minutes. Transfer to a wire cake rack and let cool in the pan until warm, about 30 minutes. Cut and serve warm, turning each slice upside down so the pears are visible.

Index